the Waters and the Wild

The trials and tranquilities of a journey on Ireland's waterways

Gwen Wilkinson

MERRION
PRESS

First published in 2023 by
Merrion Press
10 George's Street
Newbridge
Co. Kildare
Ireland
www.merrionpress.ie

978 1 78537 449 4 (Paper)
978 1 78537 450 0 (Ebook)

A CIP catalogue record for this book is
available from the British Library.

Typeset in Sabon LT Std 11.5/16 pt

Cover design by kvaughan.com

Merrion Press is a member of Publishing Ireland

MIX
Paper | Supporting
responsible forestry
FSC® C021394
www.fsc.org

CONTENTS

ATLANTIC
OCEAN

BELFAST

Lower Lough Erne

Enniskillen

Shannon-Erne
Waterway

Upper
Lough Erne

Leitrim

River Shannon

DUBLIN

Lowtown

Grand Canal

Barrow
Line

Pollardstown
Fen

Athy

LIMERICK

River Barrow

IRELAND

St. Mullins

IRISH
SEA

Minnow

The plan was simple: build a canoe and paddle it the length of Ireland along a network of rivers and canals.

In modern English, the word 'odyssey' describes a long journey or spiritual quest marked by many changes of fortune. Such voyages are elemental in the ancient Celtic tradition of *immrama* and *echtrae* – the Gaelic word *ioramh* meaning 'to row about'. These early Irish folk stories recount navigational journeys in which the hero sets out in search of the Otherworld or the Promised Land. Springing from an oral heritage, these epic tales have been passed down through generations, adapted and refined over the course of time. I have a weakness for voyage tales. Growing up, I consumed countless books about the sea and the many great oceanic adventures, from Thor Heyerdahl's Kon Tiki voyage to Dame Naomi James's triumphant tale as the first female to sail solo around the world via Cape Horn. I allowed myself to be seduced by stories of mythical islands, such as Tír na nÓg, Hy Brasil and Jonathan Swift's Lilliput. I was enthralled and terrified by descriptions of Lasconius, Moby Dick and Jaws, mythical leviathans of the deep.

I ran away with a sailor when I had just finished a degree at university. Hungry for adventure and impatient to escape the confines of life on a small island, I set off to travel the length and breadth of the world's great oceans. For most of my twenties I worked and lived on racing yachts. Sailing on the high seas was an addictive way of life – exotic and exciting, with a whiff of danger. Ocean-crossing on a boat powered by sail alone is physically and mentally challenging. Concepts of space and time took on a new import. The longest voyage I ever made at sea beyond the sight of land was thirty-eight days. The experience was immersive in the extreme. On those journeys I realised how possible it was to experience remoteness and wildness.

Then, after several years, I turned my back on the nomadic lifestyle of a sea gypsy. I hankered instead for a more stable, settled and routine existence, until what should have been a perfectly benign experience triggered an old familiar yearning. Repetitive strain injury was causing serious pain in my right arm. Fifteen years moulding steel to form objects of sculpture had taken its toll on the tendons in my wrist. I was presented with two options: have surgery or stop what I was doing. As I wavered at the crossroads, some friends came to my rescue. One fine day they bundled me into their car and took me down to my local river – the Barrow, which flows for almost 200 kilometres through the south-east of Ireland. Recently, a company had started offering self-guided canoe trips along its length. Three of us piled into a heavy open canoe and set off downstream for the day. My crewmates did the paddling, while I sat like Cleopatra in the middle of the canoe. Arcadian views of river, mountain and sky unfolded. We passed through ancient wooded landscapes that appeared to be devoid of any human presence. The low perspective and silent passage of the canoe immersed us in the river's habitat. We became absorbed in the waterscape, listening, watching and savouring the environment around us. Gently paced and physically undemanding, the voyage was the essence of slow travel. The simplicity of the adventure and the sense of escapism it invoked were revelatory. Freed from the noise and stench of diesel-engine power and the complexity of ropes, winches and bossy skippers, I was transfixed by the experience, and craved more.

Returning from the day's paddling, I rummaged out some maps and examined the Barrow's course. Like most rivers, it can be navigated only so far upstream until it becomes too shallow even for a canoe. But near the river's headwaters I noted a short, man-made waterway that would allow me to navigate all the way to the Grand Canal. Once on that waterway, I would be able to follow its course westwards across the middle of the country and arrive on the banks of the mighty River Shannon. And the journey did not need to end there. As my finger traced the river's course upstream, I encountered a junction with yet another canal: the Shannon–Erne Waterway. This restored semi-artificial waterway allowed boats to pass, as the name suggests, from the Shannon to the River Erne, arriving ultimately at the Atlantic Ocean on the island's north-west coast. In theory, a vessel could navigate a 400-kilometre journey on this inland waterway network. The desire to attempt such a voyage by canoe became irresistible.

'A common narrative of the great navigational tales, be they Greek epic, Scandinavian saga or Celtic immram, sees the hero building the vessel on which he will embark.'

A common narrative of the great navigational tales, be they Greek epic, Scandinavian saga or Celtic *immram*, sees the hero building the vessel on which he will embark. Odysseus, with Calypso's aid, took four days to build the raft on which he set sail from the island of Ogygia. St Brendan, hero of the legendary Celtic voyage tale the *Navigatio*, built himself a currach, a traditional boat composed of a lattice frame, over which he stretched cow hides tanned in oak bark and softened in butter. The idea of building my own vessel greatly appealed to me. My knowledge of canoes and kayaking was limited to a handful of brief experiences in open river canoes and sea kayaks. Commonsense dictated that I would need a light vessel for easy portage which would be strong and stable on the water, and have enough capacity to carry camping gear and supplies for several days at a time. Research led me to the plans for an open wooden canoe called a Sassafras 12. A twelve-foot (3.6m) American 'trapper'-style canoe designed for flat-water journeys seemed to meet all my needs. Its name derived from the sassafras tree native to North America and valued for its medicinal and culinary properties. Legend has it that Christopher Columbus found America's shores by following the scent of the sassafras tree wafting out to sea. Among the canoe's many virtues, according to the company's sales pitch, 'all that is required are a few common tools and the most basic woodworking skills'. I was no woodworker, so from a practical point of view this was very encouraging. In photographs she looked stunning too, a work of art that I could, at the very least, hang over the mantelpiece and admire from the safety and comfort of my sofa.

In a freezing shed on the darkest of January days, I began marking out the four rectangular sheets of plywood that would become the foundation of my vessel's hull. The thin veneers were fashioned from the okoumé tree, a hardwood species native to central Africa. Given the global concern about harvesting tropical hardwoods, I was sceptical of the need to use such wood. But okoumé is prized in marine boat construction, and especially for canoes where thin planks are forced to bend under extreme pressure. While the tree is quick to grow, the International Union for Conservation of Nature has classified it as 'vulnerable' and at 'high risk of unnatural extraction' (from human harvesting). With this concern in mind, I made an effort to acquire the wood from a responsible supplier. In Gabon, where okoumé is the main tree species, no more than 7 per cent of the natural resource can be removed annually. A French milling company claimed to source its hardwood in a sustainable manner. Their mill is also based in Gabon, where it can benefit the local economy. In a small way, this appeased my conscience about using such a valuable raw material.

Drawing out the shape of each plank was a painstakingly slow process. According to the plans, there were over eighty points of measurement, each specifying a mark to within one-sixteenth of an inch. Precision was fundamental; there was no margin of error. To add to the complexity, all the measurements were in imperial, whereas I was more comfortable with metric. I spent several days measuring, remeasuring and then triple-checking each mark. In February I summoned up the courage to cut out the planks. The saw bit through the sheets with surprising ease, and followed the contour of each plank just outside the pencil line. Cutting through the rose-pink wood released a pleasantly sweet and earthy smell. In a matter of hours all the planks were roughly hewn. When laid out flat on the workshop floor, the ghostly outline of a canoe was visible, and I felt a stirring of anticipation. Each plank now had to be carefully shaped, conforming to the pencilled measurements I had laboured over earlier. For this task, I used two hand tools: a block plane and a rebate plane. I loved working with these tools, feeling and hearing the sharp blade peel off long curls of wood. The rhythmic process of drawing the plane back and forth along the board's edge was satisfying and absorbing. Soon the planks took on their own unique shape and curve. As each task progressed, the urge to work on the project grew stronger, and I found myself spending more and more time in the workshop. What had started out as an occasional few hours here and there became days and then whole weekends.

With the planks whittled to their final shape, I was eager to tackle the next stage, bending and setting the boards into a three-dimensional form. The plans called for a 'stitch and glue' method of assembly. For this technique, the planks are literally stitched together with thin threads of copper wire, after which the seams between each lapped

joint are filled with resin, permanently bonding the canoe's hull.

I began by drilling three hundred pinholes in the precious wood, a task that felt uncomfortably counter-intuitive. Through these holes I threaded lengths of wire. Tightening the wire loops drew the planks snugly together, and the canoe's hull miraculously took on its intended form. The tension caused the wood to bend in ways that seemed to defy the laws of physics. With torn and bloodied hands, I stood back to take in my creation. She was monstrous to behold. Bristling and hostile, she resembled an alien life form, incubating suspiciously in the cold, dark shed.

The planks were no longer tactile; the merest brush past resulted in instant entanglement, as nasty wires hooked clothing and cut flesh. My confidence wavered. I quit the shed and brooded.

The gluing part of the 'stitch and glue' required working with epoxy resin, a powerful medium. Here I was back on familiar ground, having used this product liberally in my sailing days. For the glue to cure, the ambient temperature over the course of a week needed to be a minimum of fifteen degrees – difficult to achieve in the middle of March in Ireland. When high pressure moved in across the country, bringing unseasonably warm temperatures, I disappeared into the workshop. Filling a large syringe with resin, I injected the sticky substance along the lapped joint of each plank. Hours later I stumbled out of the shed, gasping for fresh air, as high as a kite on epoxy fumes. My cheeks were flushed and the pupils of my eyeballs dilated to tiny pinpricks, as though I had indulged in a narcotic binge.

A week passed. March turned into April, and it was time to take a leap of faith and remove the wire stitching. If I had followed every step correctly, the cured epoxy resin should hold each plank in position; if not, the boards would spring apart and shatter into smithereens. It felt like an age until I removed the last piece of wire, but finally a canoe was revealed. Her stems were perfectly aligned, her rebated joints were tight and evenly lapped, and her hull maintained a round and beamy curve. A few days were spent attending to the vessel's smaller details. Two water-tight bulkheads were installed at bow and stern. These sealed chambers of air would give the canoe enough buoyancy in the event of a capsize. The gunnels I fashioned from a length of European larch, and an offcut of native oak made a strong and beautiful thwart, doubling as a yoke and backrest. All that remained was a marathon sanding job and several coats of paint and varnish.

By the end of May my canoe was ready to be moved from the confines of the workshop to the great outdoors, where, at last, she could come to life. I let my gaze trace her slender shape and graceful lines: the soft curve of her gunnels sweeping gently from bow to stern; the flare of her rounded hull yielding sharply to upturned stems; the delicate cream of her narrow lapped planks, their paleness a stark contrast to the rich russet brown of her interior. Despite the many blood-soaked sacrifices, the satisfaction of creating a boat entirely by my own hands was immense. After four months' labour, I had a strong and beautiful canoe. I called her *Minnow*.

Bringing such a vessel to life opened up worlds of possibility. In the early summer of 2019, I set out on my own *immram*, launching *Minnow* from the shores of Lough Erne in Northern Ireland. The journey was undertaken in stages and over the course of several months, finishing at the tidal waters of the River Barrow in 2020. The canoe was the one constant throughout, carrying me with grace and stamina across lakes, down rivers, along canals and up shallow rills. She turned heads wherever

'Despite the many blood-soaked sacrifices, the satisfaction of creating a boat entirely by my own hands was immense.'

we went. People quickly appreciated her classical looks and elegant lines. I travelled sometimes in the company of others, family and friends who joined me for short stretches, but for the most part I journeyed alone. Like all good voyage tales, mine took me to deserted islands and wondrous shores. Along the way I encountered realms once inhabited by Celtic deities, mythical monsters and supernatural beings. As the adventure unfolded, I learned about the lives of historic female icons such as Maura Laverty, Jane W. Shackleton, Mary Ward and Lady Harriet Kavanagh, women who have left their mark on Ireland's landscape. Most of all it was the wildlife, above and beneath the water, which became a subject of endless fascination and motivation for me. Encounters with curlew, otters and dragonflies altered the course of my

creative urge and inspired the series of lino and woodcut prints featured among these pages.

What follows is the story of my journey with *Minnow*, a self-built canoe, tracing the course of water from the shores of Ulster to the island's southern coast – an illustrated tale of cultural histories that I experienced along the margins of an ever-changing landscape.

Boa Island

START

Muckross

White Island

Belleek

The Broad Reach

Cliffs of Magho

Rossigh

LOWER LOUGH ERNE

Devenish
Island

Portora Lock

Enniskillen

FINISH

UPPER
LOUGH ERNE

Wayfinding

The hollowed husk of *Minnow*'s elongated body is a potent symbol of expectation: her silent presence an invitation to venture out from these wild shores and journey ever onwards. Vivid images of Utopian worlds play across my imagination. I reach out and touch the smooth surface of the hull, which is reassuringly taut beneath my fingertips. I alone lay claim to her. She is the vessel of my dreams, carrier of my desires.

I have yet to enter the water. Sitting beside my canoe on the northern shores of Lower Lough Erne, I like to think I am biding my time, waiting for just the right moment, but really, I am stalling. Having spent the past four months shaping this canoe, bringing her into this world, I was full of impatience to take her to the water and begin our journey. Now I'm tense, nervous and riddled with self-doubt. The view before me is intimidating; an exposed sea of open water, known locally as the Broad Reach, quivers in the bright sun. The map is unsettling. Stark warnings are blazoned across the section I am about to navigate,

'Lough becomes rough in strong winds.' Even the canoe trail guides try to dissuade, suggesting that this region of the lough is 'best left to the experts'. In planning this voyage, I knew that if I was to have any chance of crossing this daunting stretch of water, the conditions would have to be perfect, and today they are just that. Last night in my tent, holding out for the weather to turn in my favour, I felt the wind die. This afternoon the air is breathless and the water as smooth as liquid silver – a benign and languid waterway with mysterious islands waiting to be explored. The time has come, so I climb inside the hull of my very small boat, take up the twin-blade paddle and begin to journey up the River Erne.

The Erne rises in County Cavan, flows northwards through Fermanagh and bends westwards through Donegal, where it empties into the Atlantic Ocean. Along its eighty-five-kilometre course, it twice crosses the jurisdictional border between the Republic and Northern Ireland. In County Fermanagh, Northern Ireland, it occupies the landscape in the form of two large lakes, Upper and Lower Lough Erne – twin bodies of water with very different personalities. The water of the Lower Lough, where our voyage begins, sits in a deep glacial trough, its stretched and curved outline shaped like the wing of a soaring sea bird. The widest section of the lough, the Broad Reach, stretches from Duff Point on the west coast to Muckross on the eastern shore, a distance of eight kilometres. Its inner curve flows around the base of the Magho Cliffs. On most days the water here is sheltered from prevailing winds and is the safest course to paddle along. However, this rare windless day means that I can explore the lough's outer reaches, a longer and more varied route. Depending on the weather and the water's many moods, it should take me roughly three days to reach Enniskillen at the top of the lough, with two nights rough camping along the way.

The first waypoint I have plotted is on Boa Island, about an hour's steady paddle from my launch site. With luck, the short distance will give me time to settle down and enjoy myself. At this moment I am anything but relaxed. Afloat now on open water in unfamiliar surroundings, I struggle to gauge distance. The shoreline is mono-featured, a dense shelter belt of trees and scrub bending low to the water's edge. The access point I'm looking for is completely obscured. After some time, I rest the paddle across the gunnels and examine the map for clues. Momentum carries us silently, effortlessly out across the water, and when I look up, I am mesmerised by the view. The increasing heat and wobbling waterscape conspire to form a mirage-like effect, tiny islands and rocky outcrops seem to hover in the air. Distant shores look so tantalisingly close. It's a clumsy exercise trying to study a large folded chart in the confines of a wallowing canoe. Frustratingly, the place I am looking for is printed right on a crease, so I ditch the map and turn my attention back to shore.

It was the island's unusual name that sparked my interest. What did the word 'Boa' mean, and from where did it originate? Looking for answers

'Rolling over Boa's stone exposed a gaping portal through which I willingly tumbled, landing with a jolt in Ireland's pagan past.'

was much like turning over a boulder to reveal what secrets lay beneath. Rolling over Boa's stone exposed a gaping portal through which I willingly tumbled, landing with a jolt in Ireland's pagan past. In ancient Gaelic, the language of the Celts, Boa becomes *Badhbh*, a word that describes a shrieking grey crow whose carrion habits were symbolic of death, war and bloodshed. Legendary texts tell of Badhbh, a powerful and terrifying goddess of war whose spirit was invoked in times of conflict. Swooping over battlefields, the goddess Badhbh would take on the appearance of a screaming grey crow, and so piercing was her cry that it drove terror into the hearts of the most courageous warriors, killing them instantly. The origin of the word is unsettling, but perhaps the narrative is a clever ruse contrived to disguise the island's secret treasures. As I approach Boa, the 'Island of the Shrieking Grey Crow', I can't help wondering if this might be some sort of test, like those experienced in voyage tales of long ago. Underneath the heavy branches of ancient ash and oak, some cattle are jostling about at the water's edge, drinking from the lough. I send the canoe into the rocky shore for a closer look. The cattle retreat in surprise, snorting and raising their tails as they scarper off through a break in the trees. I chance my luck that this must be the landing place, step out of the canoe and haul her out of the water onto dry land.

From beneath the dark canopy, I emerge into dazzling sunlight and find my way to the entrance of a small cemetery. The site is cocooned from the outside world, bounded on all sides by a riot of brambles, ferns and flowering ground elder. A black metal fence defines the plot's perimeter.

The grass within is long, lush and a bright Kelly green. A high box hedge has recently been clipped into a severe rectangular form; its presence feels at odds in this rustic, rambling space. Somewhere in the midst of this ancient burial site stand two crudely carved stones, artefacts from a civilisation that lived here over a thousand years ago. At first glance I almost miss the legendary stones. I had been anticipating some sort of official signage announcing them. Surprisingly, there is none.

My eyes rove across the burial ground and finally settle on the figures lurking inconspicuously among the many tilting headstones. From the entrance gate I follow a well-worn path over hummocked ground and confront one of the sculptures. A human figure, head and torso only, thrusting out of the ground, so compelling that, at first, I keep my distance. Although the head is overly large and primitively defined, its countenance is powerful and arresting. Flat-faced, its broad and rounded forehead draws down to a deep V-shaped chin. Its oval eyes are huge and closely set. The faint trace of pupils emphasises its challenging stare. The mouth mocks. A tongue clearly protrudes from between parted lips. The figure has no neck; its head joins directly to the upper torso. The carving is bilateral, and when I circle the stone I experience the other half. There are subtle differences in this one's features: the nose is more delicately refined, and its open mouth is ever so slightly crooked. This face is lichen-encrusted; white and grey/green blobs creep over its cheeks, eyes and chin. The effect is less threatening than its partner. Back to back, the two figures stand, their heads, shoulders and torsos fused. The carving ends abruptly at waist level. A jagged fracture in the stone indicates that it must once have been part of a taller column. Fragments of the original form lie haphazardly in the long grass beside. There's a chunk of rock – clearly a pair of hands with elongated fingers. The half-figure has been remounted on a random lump of stone, possibly even cement – surely a crude act considering the uniqueness of the artefact.

A second, smaller carved stone stands nearby. Viewed from behind, it could easily be mistaken for just another mossy headstone. The carved detail is faint and ghostly in comparison to its neighbour. I can just make out the figure's cheeks and chin, but have to search hard to find the eye sockets and mouth. Three blooms of lichen have merged into one, enveloping the human face like a creeping skin disease. Maybe this figure was never completed, or perhaps it has endured more weathering over time. I have read that this particular stone was originally discovered on a different island, Lustymore, and that it was relocated to this cemetery in the 1930s. This carving too ends at the waist, and has, at some point, been cemented to an unrelated base at ground level.

A small collection of coins accumulates at the base of its truncated form – a votive offering, but to what god, which idols, I wonder. I turn back to the larger figure in search of similar tokens. I find them at the top of the stone, between the two skulls in a shallow trough, or bullaun, filled with rainwater. There are old copper pennies, a few sterling pounds and a two-euro coin newly minted in France, embossed with an image of the tree of life and inscribed with the motto 'Liberté, égalité, fraternité'. I dip my fingers in the money pool; the water is warm, blood warm. 'A watery wound' is how Seamus Heaney described it in his poem 'January God'.

Moved by the stone's enigmatic power and mystery, Heaney invokes the spirit of Janus, a Roman god who is said to have presided over all beginnings and transitions – Janus, the two-faced idol, one face looking to the past, while the other turns to the future; Janus the god, who gives his name to the month of January. The two-faced Boa Island figure is often referred to as the Janus Stone. The Romans and the Celts would certainly have rubbed shoulders as Caesar's armies marched across Europe, but despite its will to conquer, the Roman Empire stopped short of crossing the Irish Sea. The Irish Celts were left entirely to their own devices. They had their own gods, multiple deities, male and female. Their sites of worship were located in the natural landscape, woodland groves, hilltops and remote lake islands, such as here. There are some who say the Boa Island figure is a divine representation of the pagan Celtic god Cernunnos, that the cavity, the watery wound, at the top of the figure's head was designed to receive a pair of deer antlers. Lord of all wild things, Cernunnos 'The Horned One', is a vigorous and potent masculine force worshipped by some to this very day.

I touch my fingers to his stony grey cheek, half-hoping to experience some supernatural fissure of energy. Nothing. Just the rough feel of a five o'clock shadow. Figurative works of Celtic art are few and far between in this world, which makes Boa's carved stones exceptional. Even though they have been removed from their original context, it is a wonder they have not been taken away and placed in a museum. Yet here they stand in defiance of time in this secretive place, their presence evocative and otherworldly.

The kissing gate clangs and disturbs me from a deep reverie. A family of four enters the site. They troop along the same worn path that I followed earlier, the children running ahead of the adults. Enough now, it's time for me to move on, hand the space over to the newly arrived. I steal a few hasty photographs of the stones, leave the light-filled cemetery and return to the water's edge. *Minnow* and I slither and bump over the rutted shore, enter the water and continue on our way along the Erne.

I keep close to the shoreline, as far away as possible from the main navigation channels where speedboats, jet-skis and inflatable dinghies whiz by. The canoe glides effortlessly through the calm waters, rising and falling in the gentle swell. Sallow, Purgatory, Golden, Calf, small rocky outcrops with wind-sculpted trees slip silently by, giving way to Lusty Beg and Lusty Mor, larger islands with evidence of human habitation. Ahead of me a small car ferry shuttles across the narrow channel that separates Boa and the Lusty isles. I pull in briefly near the terminal and watch the busy comings and goings. There must be something out there to draw such numbers, but the island's interiors are so shrouded from view, the attraction is a mystery. At last, I leave the safety of the shore and set out across open water, pointing *Minnow*'s bow towards Muckross Bay, where I hope to make camp for the night.

Being alone in the canoe on this infinite watery space is a thrilling and liberating experience. For the first time in a long while, I have to find my own way across an open body of water. In the years when I sailed across oceans, we relied on multiple navigational aids: physical charts, GPS, compasses and radar. Because there were often only two of us on board, I was obliged to learn how to navigate across the vast empty spaces in case the unthinkable happened to my partner and I should find myself alone. When I returned to Ireland and set up home on a mountainside, these skills were made redundant overnight and were soon forgotten. On the Erne's Lower Lough there are no dedicated paths to follow, no signposts pointing out the way and no SatNav calling out the route. Instead, I am forced to engage with my surroundings, searching out specific features – headlands, islands, rocks and beacons – to help me find my way. Earlier I was dithering and uncertain, but now I feel dormant intuitions reawakening. I begin to tune into my environment, studying the direction of swells and tracking sudden gusts of wind on the off chance that I can take advantage of their momentum. The ability to navigate from place to place over land or water is known as wayfinding. Traditional wayfinding is practised without the aid of mechanical tools or instruments. The Polynesians are masters of this art, navigating their canoes across miles of open ocean with uncanny precision. They use natural aids, such as the stars, ocean currents, wind, weather and even the flight paths of birds to help them find their way. Such knowledge and skills are not written

'The ability to navigate from place to place over land or water is known as wayfinding. Traditional wayfinding is practised without the aid of mechanical tools or instruments.'

in any books but are passed on orally from master to apprentice. While my gentle journey is far removed from epic South Pacific voyages, I am no less immersed in my environment. The experience is empowering, and fuels my spirit of curiosity. *Minnow* slices through the smooth water with silent ease. Momentum makes the paddling feel effortless, and when the dazzling whitewashed cairn looms up from the headland, I know I have arrived at last in Muckross Bay. A few minutes more and *Minnow*'s keel scrapes the harbour's sandy shore.

By early evening I have pitched the tent on a grassy patch down by the water's edge. It's a beautiful setting, and popular too, judging by the steady stream of cars rolling into the carpark as the sun begins to drop on the far side of the bay. I approach the owners of a camper van, a retired couple who are touring the country with Barney, their adventurous tabby cat, to find out if they plan to stay the night. The man is keen to chat, and the two of us stroll up and down the beach, where I humour his wild conspiracy theories. Barney is in cat heaven, claiming the sandy strip as his personal cat litter tray. Despite the assurance of my camper-van neighbours, the site is very much the opposite of 'a quiet little spot'. A constant stream of headlights sweeps the beach and illuminates the tent's interior well into the night. Most do rapid, noisy drive-bys, spinning gravel in typical boy-racer style. Others linger. Cans are consumed; I can hear them rattling on the tarmac where they have been discarded. A giddy young couple take a midnight swim. Their voices carry high and clear across the water. 'Am I a dolphin or a salmon?', the girl shrieks repeatedly. I've half a mind to get up and tell her that no such beasts exist in the Erne, that she's more likely a pike or an eel, but it would be unfair to cloud the memories the couple are creating. At some point in the early morning hours, I eventually fall asleep.

Barney the cat wakes me at dawn. The big tabby prowls around the perimeter of my tent and twangs a guy rope. Backlit by a full moon, the cat looks gigantic. Once I get over the initial surprise and confusion, I rise, dress, and start the business of breaking down camp and packing up belongings. A lone elderly male arrives and enters the water for an early-morning dip. The door of the camper van springs open and my neighbour hovers at the entrance. Dishevelled and clutching at a gaping dressing gown, he waves good morning. I wave back half-heartedly, not wishing to get stuck in strange conversations with a semi-naked man at this early hour. Turning back to watch the bay, I wolf down breakfast and burn the roof of my mouth with scalding-hot coffee. The dawn swimmer has ventured far beyond the bathing boundary. Buffeted by a lively onshore breeze, he has rolled over on his back. With arms moving in a slow, steady cartwheel, he pulls his body out into the lough. Time for me to follow suit.

Back on the water and the entire lough is mine. It's far too early for the jet-skiers, and not quite time for the chartered cruise boats. There's a handful of anglers in small clinker-style boats, but I have nothing to fear from them. The Erne is in a different mood today: it feels lively and energetic. A steady breeze comes out of the west, stirring up wavelets that smack broadside into *Minnow*'s hull. Today's destination is Rossigh Bay, a fifteen-kilometre journey following the lough's eastern shore. Again, I pass the whitewashed beacon, skirt the rocky headland and aim for distant shores across a half-moon bay. I weave a way between a scattering of small islands and rocky outcrops. Rabbit, Duck, Horse, Black Rock, White Rock, Scattered Rocks, naïve yet practical names, nothing too mysterious or imaginative here. Farther out across the water, where the lough begins to deepen, lie Gravel Ridge, Stallion Cowes and Screegan, featureless spits of land that hunker low in the water. Hostile to humans, they are home to raucous colonies of sandwich terns, black-backed and black-headed gulls who thrive on the stony habitats. These islands are designated Areas of Special Scientific Interest, and it is forbidden to trespass on them, especially during the birds' critical breeding season. Landing places are few and far between in this vast space, so I have no choice but to paddle on. Midway through the morning's journey, I round a long, thin headland and turn into Castle Archdale Bay, finding refuge in its sheltered waters. My course weaves through a cluster of modest-sized islands. These are places that once supported several families. Cleared of trees, there would have been just enough grazing to sustain a few head of cattle or a small herd of sheep. A few are privately owned retreats, but most are now deserted.

Above the water a column of birds tumbles in the sky. At first, I take them to be gulls, terns feeding perhaps. But the closer I approach, I see they are far too small to be such birds. Dropping and rising, twisting and spinning, these birds look as if they are flying for the sheer joy of it, rather than for any fundamental need. The black and white markings of their under-bodies flash dizzily. The flock continues to winnow and drift, but it is only when their noisy chatter reaches me that I realise they are lapwings – nervous, excitable, restless lapwings! Their acrobatic display is a joy to watch, and holds me spellbound on the water for quite some time. These are birds that go by many names, depending on where in the world you are. Here are just a few: peewit, plover, honeywinks, toppyup, lappy and thieve's nacket. In Ireland we know it as the philbin, a nod to King Philip II of Spain whose plumed black hat resembles the bird's fabulous crowning quiff. I shouldn't have to get excited by the sight of this once common bird. Not so long ago the lapwing was considered to be the 'farmer's friend', welcomed and encouraged to settle on meadows and pasture land. They acted as efficient pest controllers, feeding on leatherjackets, wireworms and water snails. Their numbers have declined so much in recent years that it's only by travelling to these watery margins that you have any hope of encountering them.

It's not the first time the lapwing has been taken to the brink. As a ground-nesting bird, it was vulnerable to egg hunters and collectors. Wild birds' eggs have long been gathered as a primary food source, but the practice really came into its own during the Victorian era. Plovers' eggs were highly desirable and fetched good money, 'The beautiful colour of the white being generally so much admired', according to Mrs Beeton's 1861 *Book of Household Management*. *Oeufs de Pluviers en Aspic* was a particular favourite of Queen Victoria. Teams of egg pickers stripped the nests to satisfy a seemingly insatiable demand. There are some who speculate that the practice of collecting lapwing eggs may even be a precursor to today's

Easter egg hunt; the bird's peak breeding season happens to coincide with this annual celebration. In Britain it took parliamentary legislation – the Lapwing Act (1926) – to save the bird from annihilation.

Lapwings, along with their fellow wading friends, the curlew and the snipe, have found a sort of refuge out on the Erne. The islands they occupy are designated sanctuaries managed by the Royal Society for the Protection of Birds (RSPB). Of the forty-three reserves, twelve are maintained specifically for wading birds. Of course, it isn't just a simple case of handing over an entire island to a flock of birds and leaving them at it. A cruel irony now sees the birds dependent on the very species that pushed them to the edge. It is no coincidence that the decline of the wading bird coincides with the desertion of the lough's islands. When the islands were occupied and grazed by sheep and cattle, vegetation and predators were kept in check. As soon as the last families moved off to the mainland, badgers, foxes and mink quickly moved in to take their place, and the landscape descended into a wild and woody state. Conservation of the lapwing's island habitat is now an endless and consuming task for the RSPB and its army of volunteers.

I lose sight of the lapwings as they drift inland. They will settle in fields somewhere and probe the earth for grubs, returning to their island homes before night falls. For a while, at least, the birds are safe from us blundering humans.

The canoe travels swiftly over the now smooth waters, slipping through the narrow channel that separates Strongbow from the mainland, cruising past the reed-frilled shores of Crevinshaughy and onwards to White Island. I have been drawn to this particular place by an unconventional aristocratic female, Lady Dorothy Lowry-Corry, an amateur archaeologist and antiquarian who was born in the late nineteenth century. I first came across her name at the Enniskillen Castle Museum, which I had

visited a few days earlier. Among the medieval treasures on display are several stone heads that are listed as having been donated by Lady Lowry-Corry. She came from privileged stock; her family home was Castle Coole, a large country pile on the banks of the Erne near Enniskillen. She was passionate about the history and antiquities in her native county, a trait she inherited from her father, the 4th earl of Belmore. Lady Dorothy was an unusual woman of her time. Foregoing marriage and other conventions considered acceptable to ladies of polite society, she pursued an interest in pre- and early Christian history. In time she became an acknowledged expert in her field, becoming vice-president of the Royal Society of Antiquaries of Ireland. An obituary in the *Ulster Journal of Archaeology* in 1967 remembers her as 'an indefatigable field-worker' and how she 'did not spare herself in crossing bogs and penetrating blackthorn thickets when tracking down sites'. Through her work, the historical significance of the carved human effigies peculiar to the Erne came to public light. It was she who made the first detailed studies of both the Boa Island stones and the eight stone figures on White Island, which I have come to see.

I leave *Minnow* tied fast to a pillar beneath the island's small wooden jetty and follow a muddy track through tangled hawthorn trees into a rough pasture. Meadowsweet and marsh thistle grow shoulder high, and in the centre of the field stand the ruins of an ancient church. History is layered here. At first it was a sanctuary for early Christian missionaries. Possibly a small monastery even stood here in the ninth century, but all the monks' handiwork was levelled by invading tribes, and for several hundred years, the building lay in rubble. A second attempt was made, sometime in the twelfth century, to erect another church, and the masons incorporated the old fallen stones into the new building's walls. But these, too, crumbled and collapsed with the passage of time. Roofless now, the structure's grey stonework is thickly smeared with white and mustard-yellow lichens. At some point the ruined church was encircled by a perimeter wall, whose only point of access is a slippery stile. Once inside the enclosure, I pass through the church's arched stone doorway and enter its nave. For a strange moment I feel as if I have stumbled into a bizarre identity parade. Eight stone human figures stand on the facing wall, staring back at me.

Carved in relief on rectangular blocks of quartzite, each piece is unique in size, pose and finish. Though they are not as primitive as the Boa Island figures, there is a shared resemblance in some of the facial features – the enlarged heads, wide, almond-shaped eyes and open mouths. Several of the faces have ears; some even have delicately curling fringes. Five of the standing figures wear full-length tunics, and the sculptor has chiselled feet sticking out from under their hems. Each robed figure holds a religiously symbolic object in his hands. The passage of time has worn down the carved detail, so you have to work very hard to make out what the objects are. I can just make out a crozier and a bell. One figure is seated, a book balanced in his lap. All but one of the figures are assumed to be male. The exception, the clear suspect in this odd parade, is an impish effigy, a small, semi-cloaked figure with hands resting on the thighs of its awkwardly splayed legs. Its gender is ambiguous. This disturbing carving must have come as quite a surprise to the person who first discovered it in 1844.

The figures were revealed at different times and over many years as work took place around the building. The most recent carved stone was discovered in 1958. Several were found re-purposed as building blocks in the church's wall, the significance of the carvings clearly lost on the medieval labourers. The site has never been thoroughly excavated, so it's possible that there are yet more figures buried in the earth waiting to be revealed. All eight stones have been permanently mounted against the church's interior wall in a precise linear row. A long lintel sits above their heads, offering token protection from the elements. It's a weirdly wonderful art installation. The vivid and comedic facial expressions, the flagrant pose of the mischievous hunky punk, and why exactly is that man trying to strangle two strange beasts? On a weathered sign outside the enclosure an attempt has been made to interpret the site. A vague date is suggested for the figures, somewhere between the ninth and eleventh centuries. The true origin and meaning of the stones, however, remain a mystery.

A fine drizzle begins to fall into the roofless room. I manage to ignore it for a while, but then suddenly the heavens open, forcing me to quit the stones and run for cover beneath the trees. It's only a shower, and it passes quickly. I return to the canoe to retrieve some food and water. Ducks magically emerge as soon as I settle down on the pontoon. The sun returns, hot, heavy and dazzlingly bright. The lake is wide awake now; motor boats and jet-skis career around the islands. You can hear the vessels coming long before you see them. Speed is the thing. The faster your boat can go, the better, so it seems. I have yet to see a sailing boat or meet another kayaker. In my mind's eye I summon up an image of the Vikings and their longboats travelling rapidly across the water a thousand years ago. They came down from the north, the *Dubhghall agus Fionnghall*, 'Dark and Fair Foreigners', as the Celts referred to them. They hauled their vessels overland and relaunched on the Erne, the long, slow river a riparian dream in the eyes of these skilled boatmen. When they approached these islands, did they come in stealth or with noise, I wonder? The islanders would never have seen anything quite like it – elongated hulls, lavishly decorated and rowed by up to sixty burly men. The early Christian missionaries who lived on White Island would certainly have been powerless in the face of such fearsome adversaries. Perhaps they were oblivious of the enemy approach, so secluded were the inhabitants from the world outside, assuming the vegetation was the same back then as it is today. The Vikings were on the hunt for riches, and for bodies. The raids were quick and brutal. Survivors were taken prisoner and sold into slavery. Valuables were stolen. Buildings were levelled.

The family of ducks has swum off; expecting the usual crusts of bread, they turned up their noses at my offering of cheese. The afternoon is getting on. The wind is picking

'In my mind's eye I summon up an image of the Vikings and their longboats travelling rapidly across the water a thousand years ago.'

up and the sky is clouding over. I can feel a change in the air, and it doesn't bode well. I start to worry about squalls, not wishing to be caught out on the water, where I'll be vulnerable. It's time to paddle on and find Rossigh, a safe harbour for the night. I return to *Minnow*, pull on waterproofs and untie from the mooring post, then strike out southwards, past the sprawling woods of Castle Archdale Park. For a while the sun is intense and warming. A bright-blue damselfly hitches a lift on *Minnow*'s bow and a wild bee makes busy around my canary-yellow waterproofs. But once I leave the bay and the shelter of its islands, I become exposed to the incoming squalls. I have a clear view of the heavy black clouds scudding in low and fast over the Cliffs of Magho. Beneath these clouds, the gusts will be strong and the rain intense. There is no time to linger and explore. My paddling strokes are urgent and decisive now.

The first barrage arrives, turning the water from playful glitter to steely grey while the wind intensifies to a shrill whistle. Any second now, the deluge will be upon me. I make for the shelter of a nearby jetty just in time and hide beneath its elevated boardwalk. Heavy raindrops pummel the boards above my head and the temperature drops drastically. The shower clears just as abruptly as it arrived. I emerge into the sun, but the race is on, as another menacing squall looms. It's the first time I have ever worked the canoe in these conditions. As soon as a strong wind hassles the hull, *Minnow* responds by turning her bow into the wind. I find myself continually correcting my course, and the added effort quickly tires my arms. Between all the over-correcting and careless digging of the paddle blades, I work myself into a sweaty lather. Our wake of bubbles is a hopeless zigzag trail. It's difficult to gauge my progress – am I travelling forwards or drifting sideways? Moderate concern threatens to boil over into full-blown panic. But at length I reach the harbour and, with the wind behind me, *Minnow* surfs down the breaking waves. On a fizzing cushion of bubbles, I am carried into the safety of Rossigh Bay.

Rossigh features as a waypoint on the Lough Erne Canoe Trail. The trail is a positive initiative aimed at boosting water-based activities along the river. There are helpful facilities for the adventurous paddler, such as slipways, designated areas for rough camping and, occasionally, toilet and shower facilities. The idea of a flushing loo and hot running water is very appealing after two days roughing it. Sadly, it is not to be at Rossigh, as the wash house is locked and shuttered. By late evening the place is still deserted, and it looks like I'll be spending the night here on my own, a prospect I'm not too comfortable about. If only the wind would drop, I could head out to one of the islands nearby, but white horses funnel through the short divide. Crossing it now would be far too risky. I set off on foot around the bay, hunting for a camping spot out of sight of the public carpark. The shoreline is beautiful here – a natural meadow brimming with wild flowers, creamy tufts of meadowsweet, wands of purple loosestrife, bushy mare's tail and tall bulrushes, wild angelica exploding like fireworks. When I find an orchid, all my worries are forgotten. Tiny, shy and dazzlingly white, an O'Kelly's spotted orchid hides in plain sight. Right here, among the orchids and meadowsweet, is where I decide to pitch my tent. The wind slackens off at dusk. Coots and duck venture out from hiding in among the reeds. Midges, black clouds of them, seek out blood. Despite all the fresh air and exercise, I still find it hard to fall asleep. Strange feral instincts have been triggered. Alert and twitchy to the slightest sound, I lie rigid in the sleeping bag, my over-active imagination running off its leash.

Of course, I do fall asleep, and wake the following morning to find the tent's exterior covered in slime trails. Slugs of all sizes have explored every square inch of canvas during the night. Today is my last on the Erne's Lower Lough. A short day's paddling will take me into Enniskillen, where I can stock up on food and water for the next leg of the journey. I load the two dry bags into the canoe, slide her back through the rushes and head out into the bay. Overnight the waters have calmed; the Erne is friendly once again. With the Broad Reach well behind me, the lough begins to narrow. In these parts it is roughly two kilometres from shore to shore. It's a straight run today – there are no bays to cross or headlands to round. The way will be littered with islands identical in size and shape, a waterscape characteristic of a post-glacial event. Oddly, many of them share the same names as those I travelled past earlier: Rabbit, Horse and White featuring yet again. Then Goat, Owl, Hay, Paris Big and Paris Small. Their shorelines are fringed with reed beds, and look friendly and approachable.

Early into the morning's paddle, a bird's head pops up just off *Minnow*'s bow. With a long, straight neck and semi-submerged body, it looks just like a tiny submarine propelling through the water, its periscope raised. It moves rapidly, scanning left to right, then disappears abruptly below the surface. I stall the canoe, rest the paddle across the gunnels and wait for the bird to re-emerge. Up it pops again a few seconds later, far removed from where it originally dived. I notice several more small periscopes all behaving the same way in the shallows around the reeds –

darting, diving and re-emerging. I paddle tentatively in their direction but the creatures are extremely shy and furtive. With each attempted approach, they vanish beneath the surface. Without binoculars, I can't make out what sort of birds they are, but I do have a camera that can focus in close. I click off a few quick snaps and replay the images on the monitor, zooming in on the birds' heads.

The long, spiky ear coverts and copper-coloured frill around the neck reveal the markings of the great crested grebe. While their plumage may be regal and exotic, it is the grebe's courtship display that perhaps attracts most interest. Both males and females participate equally in a rich and intricate dance, a sight I would love to see someday. For now, the breeding season is complete and these birds are teaching their fledglings how to feed, swimming and diving in pursuit of underwater prey. I linger with the grebes in the hope that they will accept my presence, but they are far too timid, and their dives and underwater swimming lead them farther and farther away.

In contrast to the lapwing, grebes are making a comeback from near extinction. In the latter half of the nineteenth century the number of great crested grebes had declined to only fifty breeding pairs in Britain and Ireland. Today, over 4,000 breeding pairs have been recorded in Britain. The cause of the bird's demise was the plume trade that gathered pace from the 1860s onwards. The ornate head feathers of the crested grebe were used to decorate hats, and 'grebe fur', the downy skin of the bird's breast, was prized for muffs and boas.

During the Victorian era it was considered the height of fashion to accessorise a garment with feathers. Feathered hats were extravagant and dazzling creations. Whole birds were reconfigured and taxidermied into bizarre parodies of themselves, to be worn as outlandish head-dresses. Hummingbirds were worn as brooches. Consider this description of an *haute couture* headpiece in the fashion magazine *Harper's Bazaar* in 1875: 'The entire bird is used and is mounted on wires and springs that permit the head and wings to be moved about in the most natural manner.'

And, of course, the most beautiful birds were the most prized. Exotic feathers became a highly coveted status symbol. But no bird was safe; herons, woodpeckers, bluebirds, owls, warblers, snipe, plover, starlings, parrots, little auks and egrets were all fair game. In 1886, globally an estimated five million birds were killed for their feathers. Plume hunters lay in wait at nesting sites and colonies. It was the nuptial plumes they were after, the birds' bright mating feathers. Whole colonies could be annihilated in two to three days – young chicks left to fend for themselves and ultimately starve. By the late nineteenth century, hunters in the US had brought the population of snowy egrets, flamingos and spoonbills close to extinction. Propaganda strove to reassure that birds were a limitless resource, and that hunting practices were humane. Other spin stories advocated that wearing feathers and whole birds brought the urban dweller closer to nature and improved societies' awareness and knowledge of bird species.

Plumes were sold by weight; one ounce was the equivalent of four to six birds. The price of an ounce of feathers in 1915 was $32, significantly more than the price of gold at the time. For a London auction in 1902 a grand total of 192,960 herons were killed for their plumes. Another sales report, from 1911, lists the species and number of bird corpses auctioned as including 13,598 herons, 129,168 egrets and 41,090 hummingbirds. This listing covered just four dealers, a tiny fraction of the European trade.

Fortunately, there were some who opposed this fashion trend, who saw through the spin and made it their mission to challenge the status quo. It took the courageous actions of three English women – Emily Williamson, Eliza Phillips and Margaretta 'Etta' Lemon – to bring an end to the plume trade and focus attention on protecting the birds whose lives were under threat.

At the age of twenty-six, Williamson founded 'The Plumage League', an all-female group who pledged never to adorn their hats or clothes with feathers. In the same year, 1889, Phillips and Lemon had co-founded a similar organisation, which they called the 'Fur, Fin and Feather Folk'. Finding common ground in their concerns for animal welfare and wildlife conservation, the two groups joined forces, and the 'Society for the Protection of Birds' was formed. Eliza, the eldest of the three, already had experience in animal welfare activism, and she took on the role of publications director. Etta was the forthright one, outspoken, fearless and occasionally contrary. Emily was something of a trailblazer; in addition to her conservation work, she also established the Gentlewomen's Employment Association, along with funding programmes to subsidise young women's education.

Initially, the society had an all-women charter, but this gender imbalance was soon righted as public awareness and support grew. For over ten years, the society campaigned tirelessly, highlighting the devastating impact on bird populations as a result of plume hunting. Their efforts were finally rewarded when legislation was passed by Westminster banning the importation of plumes and ending the use of feathers in clothing. In 1904, the organisation received a Royal Charter, and the Royal Society for the Protection of Birds, the largest wildlife conservation charity in Europe, came into being.

Away in the distance, I catch sight of a tall spire reaching high into the sky above the hinterland. Devenish Island must be drawing near, its round tower a powerful beacon to all wayfaring and water-weary travellers. On a bare hillside, silhouetted against the sky, the ruins of a once great monastic settlement commands the landscape. From medieval times, Devenish was renowned as a 'house of hospitality', a refuge and resting place for penitent pilgrims who followed the sacred ways. It's a heritage that endures to this very day. Of all the islands on the Erne, Devenish is by far the most visited. Lingering offshore, I watch a steady

'Devenish Island must be drawing near, its round tower a powerful beacon to all wayfaring and water-weary travellers.'

stream of ferry and hire boats pull into its harbour. A long, motorised catamaran, brimming with tourists, rounds the island from the Enniskillen side. I stand off and wait for it to dock against the pier. The twin jet-propelled engines churn the waters silty grey as the hulking vessel reverses, turns and finally settles to her mooring. An extended family of French visitors disembarks noisily. When all is quiet,

I tuck behind the main jetty, where a simple cutting in the bank has been carved out for kayaks and canoes. My hands and knees sink into thick sticky blobs of faeces as I clamber ashore. I curse the duck who left them there. I pull *Minnow* from the water, grab my camera and set off to explore more stones.

The atmosphere of this place contrasts starkly with my previous island visits. No wilderness here, no nettles, thistles or tangled trees; this is a fastidiously managed site. An asphalt path leads up from the shore to the church ruins. The sprawling lawns are so tightly manicured, I hesitate to step on them. Numerous weatherproof noticeboards stand at intervals along the path describing aspects of the site's history. There is even a small visitors' centre with a thin display of prints and photographs. Despite the air of controlled discipline, we are free to clamber over and about the ruins.

The island's sacred reputation is the legacy of one man – St Molaise. As a young missionary who chose to dedicate his life to promoting 'God's Greater Glory', Molaise settled himself on Devenish in the early sixth century. A monastery was established and it developed a reputation for teaching the art of writing and delicate metalwork. Following a visit to the Eternal City, Molaise had lofty ideals that the island should become an Irish Rome. Word of the saint's miraculous powers spread far and wide – he could uproot trees with a simple verbal command and halt advancing armies with a wave of his hand. Little physically remains today of the ecclesiastical domain of 'Molaise of the Lake' – it wasn't until the ninth century that Irish monks built in stone. Successive religious orders scaled up the site, adding a large cloistered priory and the slim five-storey round tower, substantial buildings of sounder longevity. So highly was the monk's authority respected throughout the land that, in brokering tribal rifts and settling disagreements, Devenish was known for a time as the 'Isle of the Assemblies'.

A single treasured artefact was discovered near the site, a small gilded case referred to as a book shrine. The Soiscéal Molaise is a tiny object crafted out of copper alloy and sheathed in decorative plates of silver. Its surface is embellished with semi-precious stones, gold interlace and red enamel. Recovered from the waters of the Erne, it sits today in a dimly lit corner of Dublin's National Museum, where it is easily overlooked. The experts say that it dates from the early eleventh century, and that a copy of the Gospel of Molaise may have been contained within the case. Book shrines were highly revered objects, and there were many who believed in their power to determine innocence or guilt and decree judgments.

In keeping with the nature of ancient sacred sites, superstitious myths cling to these stones. Before I leave the island, I can't resist a quick look at the fabled 'healing grave'. It is found inside the ruins of Teampall Molaise, a coffin hollowed from a single stone slab that is understood to possess mysterious curative powers. It is said that if a person can fit their body inside the hollowed stone and turn around three times, their back pain will be relieved. I scramble over the priory walls and meet the French family, who are trying, unsuccessfully, to take a group selfie. I offer to take their picture and am bombarded with requests to take photos with all their camera phones. Before other groups descend, I escape up the path and reach the crest of the hill. The remains of a high cross stand tall among the ancient prostrate headstones. A barbed-wire fence cuts across the ridge and a herd of suckler cows paces its length, bellowing noisily. The island's Gaelic name, *Daimhinis*, 'Ox Island', has an appropriate ring today.

Minnow and I leave Devenish and set out for Enniskillen. Skirting the island's shore, I am drawn to a curious structure half-hidden in the *Phragmites* reeds. From a distance and my low vantage-point, it looks like a bird has built a very large, elaborately shaped nest right on top of a fence post. I draw the canoe in closer to get a better look. Perched on a stout wooden post, there is indeed a large tubular nest, but I see now that it is man-made. The hollow form has been moulded out of galvanised mesh wire, which has then been padded out and stuffed with reeds. The whole unit sits roughly a metre above water. Farther along the shore I encounter several more similar nest poles. Each is unoccupied, and I am mystified about what bird would find them appealing. It is several days later that I learn their purpose. More accurately described as 'hen houses' or 'nesting tunnels', their function is to provide wild duck with a safe nesting place out of reach of predators. According to the Devenish Wildfowlers and Conservation Club, who have installed thirty such tunnels around the area, it is the first experiment of its kind in the UK, and it has, so far, proved successful. I can't help thinking that the principle of the nest tunnel bears an uncanny resemblance to Devenish's monastic round tower, the principle of finding safety from the enemy by gaining height – and don't forget to pull the ladder up after you.

In past times it was the Vikings who were the most feared enemies on these waters. Today it is the mink who rule the river, another foreign invader meting out a reign of terror all along the Erne. A semi-aquatic carnivore, the mink must have access to slow-moving fresh water, and the Erne could not be more ideal. Their natural instinct is to surplus kill. When faced with a bounty of prey, a mink will kill everything, despite having satisfied its appetite. This sly, casual killer has had a devastating impact on the river's populations of ground-nesting birds. Curlew, lapwing, corncrake, terns, duck, coots, moorhens, even swans are all vulnerable prey. Mink are partly to blame for the demise of the common scoter duck, a bird once prolific on the Erne, but now extinct.

The pelt of the American mink is highly prized in the fashion industry. The fur is lightweight, decadently soft and has a unique sheen. A full-length coat can fetch as much as $50,000. The first mink farms, specialising in breeding captive American mink, were established in Ireland in the 1950s. Through deliberate release and accidental escape, the mink entered our ecosystem with devastating consequences. The solitary predator was quick to adapt to its new habitat and settled itself at the top of the food chain. In 2010, under the cover of darkness, a group of animal rights extremists broke into a farm in neighbouring County Donegal, armed with bolt cutters, and released 5,000 mink from their cages into the wild. The event was

regarded as an environmental disaster. Nowadays mink farming is banned in fourteen EU states, and is set to be phased out in Ireland. Meanwhile, the mink exacts its revenge, shattering the native wildlife's fragile equilibrium.

I paddle on, skittering past Friar's Leap, after which the

riverbanks close in tightly. The narrow channel is filled with boats of all shapes and sizes. These paddling conditions are new to me, and my senses are on high alert as I join the flotilla. Ferries crammed with tourists churn the water to a froth. Above the strum and stench of diesel engines, pre-recorded tour commentaries play out of loudspeakers. Others belt out techno music, and within the plexiglass cabins I see a barman pulling pints and serving cocktails. Strange voices float across the water: French, German, Dutch and the slow Fermanagh lilt. Jet-skis rip by. Two black police boats rumble past. *Minnow* pitches and rolls in the confused waters. I feel as vulnerable as a cyclist in rush-hour traffic. Instinctively, I make for the riverbank, darting in and out of reed clumps like a nervous coot. A part of me wants to turn tail and skedaddle back to the Lower Lough but it's too late now. Enniskillen rises out of the Erne – a city of glittering buildings straddling the river and guarding the entrance to its upper reaches. It's here I'll break my journey, rest up and restock before taking on the next stage. My journey on the Lower Lough ends as, frazzled and dishevelled, I pull into Portora – *port-na ndeora*, the landing place of tears.

UPPER LOUGH ERNE

START
Enniskillen
Bellanaleck
Belle Isle
Trannish Island
Govindadvipa (Inish Rath)
FINISH
Crom
Inishfendra
Gad Island
Shannon-Erne Waterway
Belturbet

Castaway

There's a fork in the river ahead. I let the canoe drift while weighing up which course to take. Rising up in front of me is Inis Ceithleann, Kathleen's Island, around whose shores the River Erne eddies and swirls. According to legend, the wounded warrior princess Kathleen met her death on this small nub of land. Pursued by the enemy, she dived into the turbulent river and attempted to swim the channel, but even the ablest swimmer would struggle to make it to the other side. The town of Enniskillen now engulfs the island from which it takes its name. An urban panorama spreads out beyond the riverbanks – church spires and communication masts, office and apartment blocks, factory units and housing estates. But I'm not here to take in the view; I'm trying to figure out the safest route around the island to reach the Upper Erne. Neither option looks appealing. The west passage, the main boating channel, is wide, deep and agitated. The eddying water indicates a powerful current as the river passes through a pinch-point. The surface is churned by a steady stream of boat traffic. I'm still not comfortable sharing confined waterways with engine-powered vessels, so I opt for the route less travelled, the river's east passage, accessible only by tiny craft such as mine. Decision made, I paddle smartly past the heavily fortified police station and wade upstream. Friendly grass banks give way to hostile concrete walls. I have a moment of doubt and hesitation before entering a narrow gully. The way narrows almost to the point of being impassable as it disappears under the town. Dark, chilly and smelly, this is definitely not the sort of experience I was expecting on my kayaking adventure. Even so, it's thrilling, in a post-apocalyptic kind of way. I pass from light to shade as road bridges and pedestrian walkways crisscross overhead. It's a tight squeeze for my long canoe. I weave around pillars, bridge supports, submerged traffic cones and rusting supermarket trolleys. Traffic is heavy on the streets above us: gears crunch, diesel engines rev, heavy loads make the foundations tremble. A multi-storey car park abuts the waterway and a driver does a double-take when our paths almost collide. Just when it all starts to feel a little too surreal, I re-emerge into the light on the far side of the town.

'Whoever controlled the waterway controlled Fermanagh, and the powerful Maguires ruled the kingdom for almost 200 years.'

Rounding the island, I hove to beneath Enniskillen Castle with its watchful towers and fluttering Ulster flag. A long time ago the Maguire dynasty controlled the Erne, patrolling the river with a private navy of 1,500 boats. The family built a castle on Inis Ceithleann in the fifteenth century. From this strategic overlook they controlled all passing trade and traffic. Whoever controlled the waterway controlled Fermanagh, and the powerful Maguires ruled the kingdom for almost 200 years. The family were patrons of the arts, and the rooms and corridors of their keep were filled with poets and musicians. Supremacy came at a high price, however, and the stone ramparts tell an exhausting tale of battles lost and won, retribution and betrayal. Against the backdrop of the Anglo-Spanish War, Ireland was regarded as strategically important, and the English Crown was determined to bring it under its control. In the space of 100 years, the castle was captured nine times, and demolished and rebuilt several times over. Ultimately the Crown was victorious and the Maguires' reign was eventually broken. A new broom sweeps clean. The castle was rebuilt and a garrison added, resulting in the present turreted building referred to now as The Watergate.

Trouble was never far away; deep social divisions percolated down through the centuries. Cutting a long story very short, things came to a head on 8 November 1987, Remembrance Sunday, a memorial day held to commemorate those who served and died in the First and Second World Wars. The ceremony was about to commence when a bomb exploded. Eleven people were killed and sixty-three people were injured. The Provisional IRA claimed responsibility. The bombing marked a turning point in the province's troubled times, and spurred efforts to reach a peaceable solution. Peace is a fragile condition. It's prone to sinister undercurrents, turbulence and muddiness, much like the River Erne, which flows through the town.

On this bright and sunny morning, the waters around Enniskillen are throbbing with activity. Boats of every size and shape are heading in all directions – fishing punts, tour buses, water taxis, cruise hire boats, Dutch-style barges, pods of canoes, herds of stand-up paddle boards, and the odd jet-ski. Fittingly, Waterways Ireland has its headquarters here, in a glittering glass edifice on the river's west bank. The body is responsible for managing Ireland's navigable inland waterways. It is one of six cross-border organisations set up under the Good Friday Agreement, part of the Northern Ireland peace process. In need of kayaking trail maps, I tie up at the jetty in front of the building and make my way to reception. A member of staff is happy to oblige with my requests for certain Blueway guides, though a cloud crosses her face when I blurt out my intention to paddle solo across Ireland from north to south. She asks me to wait in the lobby and disappears upstairs. I kick myself for telling her, not that I need official permission to do what I want to do. The employee returns with an armful of maps and kayaking guides. She presents me with a 'goodie' bag, containing a baseball hat, a waterproof phone pouch and a floating key fob, and wishes me well on my journey. I skip lightly down the boardwalk and slide into the river before anyone changes their mind.

The Erne writhes like an anaconda as it heads upstream away from Enniskillen. So snake-like is its course, there are places where it even doubles back on itself. Rounding bends, I find myself heading back towards the town. The experience is disorientating, when, after a full hour's heavy paddling, I'm still within the suburban limits. Traffic is busy in the boating lane, but the river is wide enough for me to travel beyond reach of the wakes. The channel narrows for a short stretch as it passes the sprawling estate of Castle Coole, a Palladian mansion of gleaming Portland stone and the ancestral home of Lady Dorothy Lowry-Corry. It's the first in a series of gentrified demesnes on the banks of the Upper Erne. A five-miles-per-hour speed limit slows down the bigger boats to a crawl, mercifully reducing the chop in the confined space. There's a punishing headwind too, and I have to dig deep with the paddle to make any sort of headway. There's another S-shaped bend, after which the wind is at last on my back, helping the canoe to glide effortlessly through the water. At the riverside village of Bellanaleck, I pull in for some much-needed rest.

Once I get underway again, the river takes on a very different character, as its one true channel splinters into a labyrinth of waterways. Lesser tributaries feed into the flow. Outflows lure me into wide bays and hidden loughs. The watery maze takes me to all points of the compass, including several dead ends. There are channel markers but no signposts as such. Every few minutes I refer to my map for reassurance that I'm still on course.

My destination is Belle Isle, one of the largest islands on the river's Upper Lough. So far, I haven't had the chance to stay on an island, despite an abundance, since all are either privately owned or wildlife sanctuaries. The fear of being weatherbound has also put me off. Tonight will be my first island sleep-over, although I don't intend to 'rough it' quite yet. When I was planning this section of the voyage, Belle Isle appealed as a gentle introduction to island living. It is billed as private and exclusive, and guests can reserve a room either in the lavishly furnished castle, complete with four-poster bed, or, as in my case, in the less formal courtyard apartments.

The light fades as I approach the island. Diverging from the main waterway, I follow a quiet rivulet up to the estate's private jetty. A short distance from where I pull the canoe ashore is a small bronze plaque. Mounted at ground level, it is easily overlooked. The panel's inscription notes the maximum water level of the Upper Lough, '153 feet' (46.5 metres). When the water exceeds this level, the Erne will overflow, flooding the surrounding countryside. Some records recall the Erne travelling as much as three kilometres inland, flooding homes, stranding livestock and washing away crops. 'In summer the Erne is in Fermanagh, in winter Fermanagh is in the Erne' is a familiar old catchphrase in these parts. In the late nineteenth century efforts were made to tame the river once and for all. There were dredging and draining projects, and a series of barrages and locks were installed at strategic points. The lock at Portora, below Enniskillen, now controls the water level in the Upper Lough. Much farther downstream, at Ballyshannon, there's a hydroelectric dam. The obscure little plaque at Belle Isle is a subtle reminder that the river on which I travel is no longer truly wild and free.

A long tree-lined avenue leads up to the doors of the stately castle with mullioned windows and walls softened by Virginia creeper. The 'castle' part is a narrow five-storey tower that looks barely a century old. The duke of Abercorn bought the ruined estate some years ago and set about restoring the buildings and landscape to their former glory. Belle Isle now earns its keep as an exclusive island retreat. Here you can play out the role of a country squire, fishing, shooting and hosting lavish dinner parties in the lofty Grand Hall. There's a party already in full swing when I arrive at reception. Dublin-registered SUVs are parked in the forecourt. A group of men saunter around the flagged patio, swirling brandy snifters. Cigar tips glow in the half-light. Having checked in, I am shown to my rooms in the stableyard.

Very early in the morning there's the sound of car doors slamming and engines echoing around the courtyard. Fishing expeditions make an early start at Belle Isle. I take full advantage of the late-morning checkout, luxuriating in soft furnishing, basking in hot running water and putting the electrical appliances through their paces in the self-catering kitchen. After breakfast I follow a way-marked trail that weaves around the island, over meadows, through woods and along the water's edge. It is late afternoon when I relaunch the canoe. The peaty water is silky smooth, and warm where it flows past the jetty. In no particular hurry, I make a slow circumnavigation of the island. Overall, the estate encompasses eight islands, and is a designated Area of Special Scientific Interest. Unusually for a grand estate, there is a lovely wildness about the place: natural habitats of rough meadows, broad-leaved woods and deep reed beds. Light-touch management has made it a haven for wildlife, particularly for red squirrels, pine martens and peregrine falcons.

But it's what lies beneath the water that attracts visitors here. Erne pike are famous throughout the world. Anglers from far and wide travel to pit their wits and rods against them. The slow-flowing river is a prime

'All along the Erne, fishy tales are told of enormous pike devouring great crested grebes and even the occasional mute swan.'

habitat for these fresh-water predators who lurk in the shadowy depths, waiting to pounce on their prey. They grow big on these waters, regularly surpassing thirteen kilograms. Pike capture the imagination. Masters of the inland-waterways food chain, they have a tendency to bite off more than they can chew, often choking to death on fish too big to swallow. All along the Erne, fishy tales are told of enormous pike devouring great crested grebes and even the occasional mute swan.

When the time comes to turn away from Belle Isle's shores, the Upper Lough reveals itself and stops me in my tracks. Flat calm water mirrors the sky. An intense azure blue is seamlessly reflected in the ripple-free water. Every cloud in the sky is perfectly mimicked on the lough's surface. The thin horizon is a shimmering mirage, wavering between barely there and not there at all. It's almost impossible to tell which way is up. For a surreal moment, I have the impression that I'm kayaking through the sky. The gently wallowing canoe intensifies this mind-bending illusion. With only the splash of the paddle to anchor me in the correct universe, I venture out across the breathless blue space.

The lough stretches out ahead for a distance of fourteen kilometres. In contrast to the Lower Lough, it has no defined shape, the main shoreline being irregular and frayed. When I studied the map earlier, I counted at least fifty islands, a bewildering archipelago of various shapes and sizes. Some are as small as tennis courts, others big enough to graze herds of cattle, sheep and goats. Their topography is soft and rounded, with meadows gently sloping down to the water's edge. I abandon my default tactic of hugging the main shore and decide to island-hop along the middle of the lough.

For several hours I travel through a kayaking paradise. With time on my side, I freely explore islands, harbours and semi-submerged wrecks. Drifting along, it's the first time I have felt able to relax and enjoy canoeing. Not once do I have to look over my shoulder to see what the weather gods are planning to throw at me, and there are endless places for me to hide and escape from speeding boats.

I don't plan to travel far today, just to Trannish Island, about midway up the lough. The island is uninhabited, and, though it is privately owned, it does welcome overnight campers. The owners have told me that access to the island is indicated by a totem pole. Having almost circled the island without any sign of a pole, doubt creeps in, and I wonder if I'm even in the right part of the lough. There's a faint possibility of something on a headland, but it could just be a telephone pole or a dead tree. Drawing closer, I feel a wave of relief as I start to make out a series of shapes carved into the wood – it's definitely a totem pole.

The bothy cottage and campsite are hidden from view behind a thick hedgerow. Ordinarily the place would be filled with scout and kayaking groups, but tonight I have the island to myself. I can finally realise a long-held fantasy: as a castaway on a deserted island. However, it appears I am not entirely alone; there are cattle here too, and this is unwelcome news. The designated camping area is splattered with suspiciously fresh cowpats. Clearly the beasts can come and go as they please. The small paddock is accessed by several gates, all of which are standing wide open; one has rotted off its hinges and collapsed into a briar patch. Mindful of horror stories in which cattle rampage through campsites, I spend the best part of an hour barricading myself in, and relax once I'm certain the cattle won't invade. In the evening, I carry my stove, pots and pans down to the shore, and cook at the foot of the totem pole.

Totem poles are traditionally associated with indigenous communities of the North American Pacific. Their decorative carvings are an expression of a particular tribe's cultural heritage, usually depicting animals, people and family legends. The Trannish totem pole is a towering vertical creation, standing at least ten metres tall. Its surface is carved with primitive animal figures – a deer, a boar, an owl and a fish – whose symbolic meaning is rooted in pagan Celtic culture.

Early Irish myths and legends emphasise the deep spiritual connection pagans felt with the natural world. Metamorphosis, in particular, is a familiar theme. Shapeshifting was a dark and mysterious art practised by the druids and sorcerers. Some exercised this supernatural ability to harness the spirit and power of the chosen animal, while others abused it, using it as a form of punishment and entrapment.

The mythical tale of Tuan mac Cairill describes an ancient recluse, the sole survivor of the Muintir Partholóin, the first settlers of Ireland. Wretched and wild, hiding in caves around Ulster, Tuan discovers the power to change his body into animal form, enabling him to live for centuries and witness successive waves of invasion. When the Nemeds arrive, he takes on the form of a stag, evading capture by running with a herd. When the Fir Bolgs come, he takes on the guise of a boar and hides in the woods. And when the Tuatha Dé Danann land, Tuan transforms himself into a hawk, taking to the skies. With the arrival of the Milesians, he becomes a salmon. In this form he survives in the rivers and lakes until he is caught in a fisherman's net and is eaten by the King of Ulster's wife, who, nine months later, gives birth to Tuan, reborn in human form.

In the rousing *Song of Amergin*, the Milesian bard, Amergin, invokes the spirit and power of the animal world and the elemental forces of nature, as his people march into battle against the Tuatha Dé Danann:

I am a stag of seven combats.
I am the eagle on the rock.
I am a strong wild boar.
I am a salmon in the water.
I am a lake on the plain.
I am the God who puts fire in the head.

The Trannish Island totem pole exudes a similar energy.

From where I sit on the island's elevated shores there is a wide view of the lough, now empty, quiet and still. I can make out no signs of life even on the mainland; there are no farms or roads in sight, let alone a village or a town. Living the life of a castaway is a concept I find compelling. To be cut off from the mainland, without access to electricity, running water and heat, presents itself as terrifying and liberating in equal measure. Daniel Defoe's *Robinson Crusoe*, the story of a young man shipwrecked and stranded on a deserted island for twenty-four years, was so acclaimed when it was published in the early eighteenth century that it sparked an entire literary genre – Robinsonade. From classics such as *Lord of the Flies* and *The Swiss Family Robinson* to J.G. Ballard's contemporary dystopian tale *Concrete Island*, themes of personal responsibility, the human condition and social dynamics are creatively explored. Other popular narratives focus on manly heroes from real life – characters who are swashbuckling, like Alexander Selkirk, or gritty and grizzly, like Ernest Shackleton. Does it take a certain type of character with a particular skill set to survive alone on an island? Do our dulled instincts kick in when faced with the challenge of survival? How might a woman fair in such circumstances? If we take, for example, the true-life story of Ada Blackjack, apparently, the answer is we can manage pretty well.

Dubbed 'The Female Robinson Crusoe', Ada Blackjack, a member of the Iñupiat people, was twenty-three years old when she endured her ordeal. She was born in 1898 near the gold rush town of Nome, in western Alaska. Abandoned by her abusive husband, left penniless and caring for a child who suffered from tuberculosis, Ada was desperate for money to pay for the child's urgent medical needs. As a last resort, she responded to a job advertisement looking for an English-speaking seamstress to join an Arctic expedition. Ada took the job and signed what she thought was a one-year contract stationed on Wrangel Island, sewing and repairing the crew's survival gear. However, the ship that was due to collect the party at the end of the expedition failed to materialise. With a second winter closing in and supplies running low, three of the five members of the team set off across the ice to seek help and were never seen again. The remaining male team member died from illness and starvation, but Ada clung to life, committed to survival so that she could be reunited with her son. Though a member of an indigenous tribe, Ada had not been raised with any knowledge of hunting or wilderness survival. For three months she lived alone in the harshest of environments, teaching herself to fish, set traps, catch foxes, shoot birds and build a skin boat. She even experimented with the expedition's photographic equipment, taking several self-portraits in front of the camp. Ada was managing quite well on her own when help eventually arrived. Finding herself the centre of a flurry of media attention on her return home, Ada resisted the label of heroine, insisting she was just a mother who needed to get home to her son.

By contrast, Englishwoman Lucy Irving chose to live on an uninhabited island. The twenty-four-year-old responded to an advertisement that appeared in *Time Out* magazine, requesting a female companion to live on Tuin, a tiny atoll off the coast of Australia. Lucy and her companion, a man referred to as G, survived on the island for just over a year. Both published accounts of their experiences, and Lucy's *Castaway* was an instant international bestseller which was later adapted for the screen. Her version of events is a fascinating insight into how such an experience plays out on the mind and body. Tuin is precisely how you might imagine a tropic island paradise; white sandy beaches, warm turquoise waters and swaying palm trees. But it is a superficial paradise, where the challenge of survival was real and severe; it was unbearably hot for months at a

time, nasty biting insects infested every nook and cranny and, worst of all, it was vulnerable to drought. Sharks, snakes, stingrays and saltwater crocodiles were an ever-present threat. Nevertheless, Lucy threw herself into island life with energy and enthusiasm, learning to fish, forage for wild fruits, chop and gather firewood, cook and manage the camp's supplies. She describes how the very wildness and remoteness that first attracted her almost killed her, as a long spell of drought proved life-threatening. When neighbouring islanders happened to visit, they found the pair severely malnourished, their bodies festering with deep skin infections, close to death's door. In spite of the hardships, Lucy's memory of the experience is overwhelmingly positive, teaching her lessons of lasting value – humility, gratitude and an appreciation of the smaller things in life.

There is still some light left in the day, so I take a walk along the shoreline of the island. Down by the water's edge, piles of long white feathers litter the ground. Shed by moulting swans, there's a mixture of sizes, from small wispy head feathers to long, strong flight feathers. They cannot be the accumulations of a single bird; several swans must have been here. If swans moult their feathers all at once, does that mean several naked birds are hiding nearby? I scavenge through the debris for the choicest plumes, imagining a sort of swan beauty salon – fastidious preening, loose feathers pooling at their feet. Soon I have gathered a bunch of at least ten magnificent specimens.

I would like to think they are the feathers of the whooper swan, but it's the wrong time of year for them, so they must be from mute swans. The whoopers start arriving on the Upper Lough only in late October, migrating in groups and families, flying non-stop from their breeding grounds in Iceland and Scandinavia. The sheltered bays, quiet islands and rich pastures around the lough are a perfect habitat for the bird. They congregate and graze on areas of sward, feeding on leaves, stems and the remains of arable crops. It's easy to confuse the two, whoopers and mutes, especially from a distance. Whooper swans have a distinctive trumpeting call. A bevy of honking whooper swans is an uplifting experience, which I've been lucky to witness at home along the River Barrow, where families overwinter. Of the three types of swan that inhabit Ireland's shores, the others being mute and Bewick's, the whooper is the only one that is truly wild.

One of the world's oldest musical instruments is made from the radius bone of a whooper swan's wing. The Ulm whooper swan flute was discovered in Germany's Geissenklosterle Cave and is dated to between 33,000 and 37,000 years old. It measures 126.5mm and has been carved with three finger holes. Hollow and strong, it makes logical sense that wing bones can be turned into flutes. In China, they made flutes from the bones of crane wings, while the French used vulture's bones. After the swan flute was discovered in shards, a replica was made, using the wing bone of a mute swan. The flute was played and the music recorded for all to hear; the notes are surprisingly clear, and you would be hard-pressed to tell it apart from a modern-day instrument.

My deserted island experience isn't going to set the world on fire. I have everything I need: a tent, warm clothes, prepacked food and litres of drinking water. There is no need to forage or salvage, no urgency to plot my escape. I lie awake for hours listening to the call of a distressed or lost coot. Somewhere on the mainland a tractor turns a meadow of cut hay long into the night. It's the first time I have felt safe camping alone. How strange that I should need to isolate myself on an uninhabited island in order to find sanctuary.

As the morning unfolds, I find myself stalling and realise I'm reluctant to leave Trannish. It never occurred to me that I might want to stay put in a place for a while. The plan is always to keep moving on, and rivers in particular seem to have an inexorable draw. I push the laden canoe through the water meadow until she is afloat and then step in. The water is dead calm and the lough eerily quiet. I thank my lucky stars for another beautiful, sunny, windless day; it's also my last full day on the Erne, and there's a lot to pack in. Out of the silence comes a deep rumbling sound, becoming louder as it approaches. Thunder? But it can't be possible given the cloudless sky. Then a heavy goods lorry bursts out of the trees and hurtles across the bridge in front of me. The driver and I make eye contact, the truck's horn blasts and I wave back in reply. The canoe slips beneath the concrete arches of the Lady Craigavon Bridge; the whole structure vibrates as the truck passes overhead. The sound, just like rolling thunder, dissolves into the distance.

Govindadvipa. The unfamiliar word trips awkwardly off the tongue. You repeat it again, slowly. Govindadvipa. The language is Sanskrit, and its meaning loosely translates to 'the island of the cow herder'. The nine-hectare island once belonged to the earl of Erne, and until recently it was known as Inish Rath. The property changed hands many times through the years, until a group of Hare Krishna monks pooled their resources, secured a bank loan and took possession in 1982. The new owners established a monastic retreat and renamed the island Govindadvipa in honour of Krishna, who, in his youth, was a cowherd. The island lies just ahead, and is my first port of call this morning.

Dense reed beds encircle the shoreline, beyond which is a seemingly impenetrable wall of willows, alders and oaks concealing the island's interior. I paddle along Govindadvipa's eastern shore, searching for a pier or jetty. A small wedge of slipway juts out from the reeds. It doesn't appear to have been used any time recently, which is a bit puzzling, but I beach the canoe regardless and set off to explore.

The undergrowth is wild and tangled, and a musty smell of organic decay hangs in the air. A rough path zigzags into the heart of the island, giving way to a clearing and a modest two-storey Victorian lodge. Guinea fowl and peacocks flock about on the lawn. Startled by my sudden appearance, the giddy birds scatter and cry out shrilly. Such exotic birds are an unexpected sight in the middle of the Erne, but to the Hare Krishna they have symbolic relevance, featuring in the tales of the movement's origins.

Founded in New York in the 1960s, the International Society of Krishna Consciousness or Hare Krishna movement has core beliefs rooted in Hinduism, the world's oldest religion. Devotion is expressed through yoga, dance, song and meditation. Visitors are welcomed to the monastery, and the leaving of gifts is discretionary. I have come with offerings of brown sugar and butter, items that are listed as pleasurable to the Supreme Lord, according to the group's website.

The temple is housed in a wing of the lodge. Pairs of shoes are neatly stacked on shelves beside the entrance door. I remove mine, knock on the door and wait. Nothing. I knock again and call out, but still there is no reply. I take a deep breath and trespass over the threshold. In the hallway, an open door leads into a large room with an ornate golden altar. Unfamiliar with the etiquette of Hare Krishna, I leave my offerings on the floor in front of the altar and quickly retreat outside. I loiter on the front lawn with the now, thankfully, silent peacocks, but still nobody has appeared. The open house, the dark woods, the deserted island are mystifying and slightly disconcerting.

'The open house, the dark woods, the deserted island are mystifying and slightly disconcerting.'

An arrow painted on a board points into the woods, the opposite direction from where I have left the canoe, but out of curiosity I follow it. Dappled light falls on a plywood effigy; a young man/boy, blue-skinned, loinclothed, wrestles a wild boar. The enchanted path leads on to another shrine, more complex than the first. The blue-skinned figure features again, draping a garland of flowers over the shoulders of a young woman. A two-headed figure sits on the ground stirring a cauldron. The further I venture, the more fantastical the adventure becomes, as yet more shrines are revealed along the path. Each one is painted in vivid colours and features a blue Krishna. It's a Pradakshina path, a ritual route circumnavigating the temple. The practice is to circle each shrine, in a clockwise direction, as an act of devotion and reverence to Lord Krishna. I photograph each shrine, evidence for later in case I mistake this experience for a dream.

Back at the jetty, *Minnow* bobs in the reeds, tugging impatiently at her bowline. Our cargo is lighter now that I have removed the large bag of sugar and butter.

Any peace and serenity I feel is suddenly rudely shattered by two jet-skis hurtling past. They make several circuits of Govindadvipa, revving their engines to a high-pitched whine. I wonder how the monks meditate through such noise. A speedboat streaks by, also at full throttle, and casting a huge bow wave. The female water-skier screams with delight at the insane speed. On the mainland a farmer spreads slurry on a field, and the smell is so toxic I almost retch over the gunnels. The stench lingers in my nostrils for far too long.

The islands are large at this end of the lough. Many are divided into fields filled with grazing livestock; others are smothered in wild woody scrub. On parts of the Erne, cattle are herded into the water and swim out to the islands. Though they can manage only very short distances, apparently the beasts will do this provided they are led by a cow with previous swimming experience. It never occurred to me that cattle could swim, and I struggle to form a mental image of the scene. Nowadays farmers mostly use boats to transport their animals to and from the islands – rudimentary shallow draft vessels, flat-bottomed and fitted with a gangway at each end, similar to a roll-on, roll-off car ferry.

I've almost reached the top of the lough. Beyond this

the Erne reverts to being a proper river, a single channel, snaking up through Belturbet, crossing the border into County Cavan. The land I'm skirting belongs to the earl of Erne, whose home is at Crom Castle. Once upon a time it was considered to be one of the finest privately held estates in Ireland, a thriving, bustling place boasting its own post office and petrol station. Today, the estate is managed by the National Trust and encompasses over 700 hectares. There are rare and diverse habitats here – riparian forests, ancient oaks, wetlands, wild meadows and several islands. I'm looking forward to exploring the place and its several unusual buildings, but first I must check in at reception and claim my camping pitch.

Down by the water's edge, wind whispers through the reeds and rustles up ancient histories. Dappled light dances over lichen-coated stones. All that remains of Crom Castle is a high gable end wall, jagged-edged and crumbling. The roofless ruin is a legacy of a time known as the Plantation of Ulster – a time when the Gaelic chieftains surrendered to the Crown, had their property confiscated and settled with Scottish and English landlords. In recognition of his services to the Crown, Michael Balfour, Laird of Mount-whinney, was granted land on the banks of Lough Erne. He built himself a castle enclosed within a bawn, which served its purpose as a fortified home for almost a hundred years. The old castle eventually succumbed to a domestic fire and was left abandoned. The ruins that stand here now are not a true expression of the original plantation building. The Victorians added walls and towers in later years for romantic effect. Part ruin, part folly, it is difficult to tell where reality ends and romance begins. The view from this

'From here I can understand the unique waterscape through which I have navigated, a swarm of drowned drumlins, fittingly described as a "basket of eggs" topography.'

elevated point is arresting. From here I can understand the unique waterscape through which I have navigated, a swarm of drowned drumlins, fittingly described as a 'basket of eggs' topography. When I eventually tear my eyes away from the wide vista and return to more immediate surroundings, my attention is drawn to what appear to be the remains of a formal garden, now a symmetrical lawn at the centre of which looms a dark thicket. I trip down the ha-ha to investigate. You imagine an ancient tree to be tall, that its trunk will be solid and broad as it reaches skywards. The hunched, spreading shape in front of me does not match these expectations. I assumed it was a bush at first, several bushes merging, but, no, it is a tree, an English yew and a very ancient one at that. The Crom yews, for they are a pair, a male and a female, differ in age. The male was likely planted in the nineteenth century, but the female is thought to be, at the very least, three hundred years old, possibly eight hundred, maybe even over a thousand. That means she could well be the oldest living thing in Ireland. But it is notoriously difficult to estimate a yew tree's age: the boughs become hollow over time, making it impossible to do a tree ring count. Beneath an evergreen canopy, its boughs are heavy and ground-sweeping. A swathe of stinging nettles forms a hem around the base. A few of the branches have been pruned, offering an entranceway to the tree's interior.

When I pass through the archway, I find myself in the most unexpected space. A multitude of twisting limbs, all sinuous and chaotic. The trees rise out of mounds roughly ten metres apart. Over time their branches have reached out across the space, intertwined, knotted and fused. The limbs are powerfully tactile; I can't help but run my hands over their surface. The coloration is unexpected too. The bark is streaked in purple, verdigris and blood red. It's a tree that has to be climbed. Because I don't recall a sign telling me otherwise, I step onto the lower branches and work my way up and around the living scaffold. The experience is nothing short of breathtaking.

The ancient Celts revered the yew, not just for its longevity, but also for its apparent spiritual and mystical powers; the yew was one of five sacred trees brought to Ireland from the Otherworld. The cathedral-like canopy of a giant yew tree was an ideal space for pagan ceremonies and clandestine meetings. Under Brehon Law, the tree was afforded protected status. Yew wood is very fine-grained, and was the preferred choice for druids' staffs. In medieval times it was favoured for making the deadly English longbow. An old photographic print in Crom's archives shows the two trees tightly pruned, with all their lower branches propped up on stakes, almost two metres off the ground. A gravel path winds in and around the base of the trees. The effect is like a huge marquee, and it is said that, back in the nineteenth century, parties of up to two hundred people would regularly dine beneath it.

A path leads away from the yews and ruins, stretching across a rolling meadow and disappearing into a shaded wood. Glimpses of the lough flash between the tall trunks of oak and beech trees, a fork in the path peeling away and leading down to the shoreline. At the end of the track an enchanting little house overlooks the water. It's small, two storeys, and built of stone, with a slipway sloping from the ground floor all the way to the water's edge. It's a boathouse – but far from the average boathouse. The slate roof is steeply pitched and the gable end finished with scalloped wooden fascia, painted navy blue. A bay window with ornate glass work offers panoramic views of the water. The top floor would have been comfortably furnished for afternoon tea, the interior walls decorated with models of sailing yachts, trophies and maritime artworks. The ground floor is an open space where, presumably, the boats were stored.

The earls of Erne were keen yachtsmen, and for a time the boathouse was the home of the Lough Erne Yacht Club. It would have been the venue for many spectacular regattas and boating displays. The wealthy and the privileged classes joined in from the neighbouring estates of Florence Court and Castle Coole. It's easy to picture the jolly scene of young ladies, bonnets tied with silk scarves beneath their chins, milling about on the terrace with the gentlemen decked out in boldly striped blazers and straw boaters, keen to demonstrate their prowess at rowing and sailing races. A browse through old black-and-white photographs shows an impressive parade of oar, sail and steam vessels gliding around the bay. The great bulk of the *Eglington*, Lord Erne's paddle steamer, dominates the scene, and floating alongside is *Firefly*, a smaller steam launch. The tall masts of *Zephyr* and *Breeze*, two fast-racing yachts, rest at anchor. Nimble sailing dinghies, 'colleens' and 'fairies' hurry to and fro. Gigs, wherries and cots are moored abreast in the shallows.

From the terrace, a paved stone slipway dips down to the water's edge. Moored against the jetty is a pitch-black rowing boat with unusual lines, an Erne cot. I've been hoping to see one since I set out on the Upper Lough. This cot is a big beast of a boat, almost twelve metres from bow to stern, and wide too. It sits low in the water, and seems to be flat-bottomed. The squared-off bow and stern give it a rustic appearance. Two-thirds of the boat is taken up with seating, long benches running parallel to the gunnels. There are two sets of oar locks.

Long before there were roads and bridges in these parts, the Erne cot was the main form of transport. Such boats served as passenger ferries and cargo vessels. They could even carry livestock, including cattle, sometimes up to twelve animals at a time, sheep and ponies too. Because it has a flat bottom, the cot can navigate the shallowest margins of the river. In some cases, it was even hauled overland with its cargo still on board, the flat bottom acting as a sleigh. As the roads improved, the cots fell out of favour, and knowledge of their construction almost disappeared. There has been a revival of interest recently, with the Lough Erne Heritage Group established to preserve the tradition of the Erne cot, along with other traditional boats. The boat moored here appears to have been built relatively recently, part of an EU-funded cross-border project, according to a tiny plaque riveted to the gunnel.

The path flits by the 'new' Crom Castle, a Disneyesque creation that defies imagination. Vistas of the water are thrown open briefly. In shallow bays where there is no boating traffic, mute swans linger, moorhens and their chicks embark on epic journeys. A pair of ravens, concealed in the tree canopy, honk loudly. A kestrel balances in the air, dips a wing tip and falls away. A red squirrel streaks through the upper branches. Because the reds appear to thrive at Crom, wildlife experts have been studying them closely to find out why. Aside from the estate being an ideal habitat, researchers have also noticed a marked absence of grey squirrels in the area, the pox-carrying grey being the red squirrel's nemesis. A theory has developed that the secret to the red's success here may be linked to the pine marten. While both colour types appeal to the pine martens' diet, field work at Crom has noted that grey squirrels dominate the pine martens' menu. The reds, being more vigilant than the greys, are less likely to be killed and eaten by the pine marten. It seems an unlikely alliance, but in practice it appears to work well at Crom.

The path completes its loop, returning to the harbour and camping grounds. *Minnow*'s slender hull chafes against the pier as the river presses heavily on her side; the current is noticeably stronger at this end of the lough. A solo kayaker comes into view, paddling steadily upstream. The bearded boatman pulls into the quay beside me and we fall into conversation. Steve is shepherding a group of teenagers who are kayaking around the lakes as part of their Duke of Edinburgh Award.

'Where are they all?' I ask.

'Oh, they're all lost.'

I'm surprised by his nonchalance.

'And you're OK with that?'

'Oh aye. It's good for them to get lost and find their own way back. Character-buildin', like.'

'A rite of passage.'

'Aye.'

We smile knowingly.

Steve admires my canoe and seems impressed that I built her myself. And then he asks the unthinkable.

'Can I take her out for a spin?'

This is a difficult one for me – I'm very possessive of my canoe. No one but me has ever sat inside her. I give Steve the once over; the man's about twice my size.

'OK then, but there's no guarantee you won't be swimming ashore!' I let the statement hang.

Steve settles his bulk in my canoe. He paddles it out into the middle of the river and puts it through its paces; reversing, turning sharply, side-stroking, paddling very fast and rocking her violently. I pace up and down the jetty, barely able to watch in case *Minnow* snaps like a twig and sinks to the bottom. Eventually Steve returns, delighted with the experience and singing the canoe's praises. For a brief moment I glow with inner pride.

'So where are you plannin' on headin' next?'

'Oh, you know, just a few days exploring the islands around here, maybe.'

I am hesitant to explain my ambitious plan, that I want to keep going, on across Cavan and Leitrim until I reach the Shannon, and then continuing along the Grand Canal and on down the River Barrow. He'll think I'm completely daft. But, of course, I can't help blurting it out. Steve doesn't even raise an eyebrow. I may as well have said 'I'm just popping down to the shop to buy milk.' As an experienced expedition canoeist, he is full of advice, and is generous with it. He demonstrates different paddle strokes to get me out of tricky situations, and makes me repeat the manoeuvres until they meet with his approval.

In due course, Steve's 'lost sheep' begin to arrive. The first canoe is paddled by two teenage girls who look exhausted, yet still have enough energy to smile and joke when they pull ashore. More canoes arrive, travelling in from all directions. It turns out everyone got lost at some stage. They all have VHF radios, mobile phones of course, and there are two other experienced expedition leaders patrolling the waters. But each canoe team is still encouraged to figure out their own way from A to B. For most, it's their first time canoeing and camping, and though they may have lost their way and are worn out by the ordeal, they are clearly enjoying themselves. The campsite is kept awake long into the night with their banter and levity.

There's an early start for me down at the slipway, stowing bags and supplies and pulling on rain gear. On the opposite shore lies Inishfendra, a small island wooded with ancient oaks that are home to a very large heronry. A recent head count noted at least sixty herons nesting in the trees. They're such a ubiquitous sight on my watery journey that I take them for granted, rarely giving herons a second glance. Perhaps it's their drab colouring, a dowdy grey, that fails to inspire; colourful birds always garner more attention. Or maybe it's their slightly melancholic air, as they stand motionless, hunched and solitary. Whatever the reason, I've just never really bothered to consider them until now, but the idea of a heronry interests me.

When I dig about for information on herons, some interesting and surprising truths are revealed. They are violent and efficient killers. Small fish are swallowed head first; larger prey are taken back to the shore, where the heron beats them to death. They are known to eat small birds and hatchlings, which they kill by drowning, suffocating or breaking their necks. But they also have a tender side. Their courtship rituals are drawn-out events, during which prospective partners caress each other with their bills. Once the female has made her decision, the male will offer her a stick, which she will incorporate into her nest, sealing the deal. On Inishfendra the herons have built their nests high up in trees. They'll use the same nest year after year, adding to it over time until it becomes too heavy and collapses.

A heron's Gaelic name is *corr éisc*, 'fishing crane'. Informally, they are known by several other names – long Mary, bog Nora, rough Sheila and throat Juny. The Celts knew the heron as the guardian of the treasures of the Otherworld and immortalised the bird in the legend of *The Crane Bag*. The story tells of a young woman named Aoife, who is turned into a heron by a jealous love rival and cursed to be a slave to Manannán mac Lir, Lord of the Otherworld, for two hundred years. When the bird died, Manannán had a bag made from its skin and filled it with his most treasured possessions. It became known as the Crane Bag, and the items it contained were said to have extraordinary magical powers. Among the many mysterious articles were the sea god's knife and shield, the King of Scotland's shears, Goibniu the blacksmith's knife-hook, the King of Lochlainn's helmet, and the bones of

Asal's pigs. The contents of the bag could be seen only in accordance with the ocean tides. If you opened it at low tide it appeared to be empty, but if you opened it at high tide its wondrous secrets were revealed.

In the great outdoors, herons have few predators. But there was a time when they were hunted birds. Heron-hawking parties were popular and exciting events. As an exclusively royal game bird, they were protected under law by Henry VII and Henry VIII. Those who breached the rule were penalised with a hefty fine. In Scotland the punishment was severe; a first-time offender received a prison sentence, but a repeat offence resulted in amputation of the culprit's right hand. Falcons were specifically trained to hunt and kill herons, which were not their natural prey. There were strict rules governing who could fly what type of falcon – a gyr for the king and a peregrine for a prince. The birds of prey were directed along the riverbanks to flush out their quarry, and as soon as a startled heron took to the air, the falcons would mob and take it down. Roast heron was a favourite dish in medieval times, forming the centrepiece at lavish dining spreads. Heron chicks and fledglings were considered delicacies.

I turn away from Inishfendra and strike out across open water. Out in the middle of the bay is an island folly begging to be explored. I had caught sight of it several times from the mainland on my walk around Crom the previous day – tantalising glimpses of a fairy-tale tower crouched on a knuckle of rock. A strong wind funnels between two islands, whipping up a nasty little chop. If there's one thing my canoe doesn't do well it is point into the wind; because of the high freeboard, the wind catches her easily and pushes the hull broadside. Recalling Steve's advice, I move the drybags into the bow and shift my weight forward. The effect buries the bow and helps keep the canoe pointing straight into the wind and waves.

It seems to take an eternity to cross the short stretch of water, but at last I break through into the calm waters of the leeward shore.

Heaving with exertion, I rest a moment and let the canoe wallow. Underneath, a mass of pondweed sways hypnotically in the river's undercurrent. I dip the paddle lightly and glide across the undulating mass up to the steps of Crichton Tower. Wild sallies, purple loosestrife and rustling reeds sprout from the rocky outcrop. The tower sits on a raised man-made platform. The circular two-storey structure is complete with tall battlements, and built of cold, rough stone. The windows share the same ornate detail as the bijou boathouse on the mainland. The architecture is a confusing mix of genres. I've read in its description that newly wedded couples, tenants of Crom, were gifted a night in the tower. With its dark, damp and spartan interior, it seems to me a very lonely and sad place to spend your honeymoon night.

The tower never served any real purpose; it had no military or strategic role, and nobody ever lived in it. It's known as a 'famine folly'. Charity in the form of handouts was disapproved of in the dark days of the Great Famine. Instead, construction projects were initiated by governments and the wealthy elite, employing starving tenants in laborious tasks, building estate walls, screens, obelisks, follies and other quaint structures.

Time to move on, leave the Erne behind and make my way to the mouth of the Woodford River.

SHANNON—ERNE WATERWAY

Upper
Lough
Erne

START

Ballyconnell

Aghalane

Belturbet

Ballinamore

Lough Garadice

Castlefore

Lough Scur

Haughton's
Shore

Keshcarrigan

Leitrim

Kilclare

FINISH

Fliuch

The longer I study the map, the more I realise that this leg of the journey is not going to be as straightforward as first assumed. To get from the River Erne to the River Shannon, I must travel along a diverse navigation system called the Shannon–Erne Waterway. The route will take me westwards, up and down two small rivers (Woodford and Yellow), across some lakes, along canals and through sixteen locks. In summertime it can be busy, with vessels travelling in either direction. On the Erne there was plenty of space for everyone, and I could easily avoid the main boating channels; here, on this mostly narrow waterway, there will be nowhere to hide. I try and take comfort from the fact that canoeists are welcomed and encouraged to explore this stretch of waterway. A lot of effort and money has gone into making the route paddle-friendly; slipways, egress and access points at locks have been added in recent years, and there's even a white-water section for the thrill-seekers. Waterways Ireland has produced a handy 'Blueways' trail map for anyone setting out in a canoe or stand-up paddleboard. The map breaks the seventy-kilometre journey into bite-sized chunks, with daily paddling distances suggested and practical facilities – toilets, showers and campgrounds – listed along the way. All going according to plan, the journey should take me four days. But first I have to figure out how to leave the River Erne and get onto the Woodford River.

A fine drizzle fills the void. It's not quite rain – no drops as such – more like mist, but slightly heavier. My light showerproof poncho just about deflects the moisture. Eventually I find the two channel markers that indicate the Woodford River and the start of the Shannon–Erne way. The river worms through flat marshland, its shoreline smothered in dense reed beds. The only conspicuous landmark is the kiln tower of a nearby cementworks plant, a grim piece of engineering whose presence is overwhelming. For a while the waterway traces the border between Northern Ireland and the Republic. Effectively, I am paddling through a no-man's land, a novel experience that distracts my thoughts as I huff and puff upstream. The physical river acts as barrier and buffer zone between two countries, a liminal space where complex issues of place, power and identity play out.

'The physical river acts as barrier and buffer zone between two countries, a liminal space where complex issues of place, power and identity play out.'

As frontiers go, the Northern Irish border is relatively new, created a century ago when the island of Ireland was partitioned. It came into being out of a long, intense political and social struggle. At the height of the 'Troubles', the practice of making roads and border crossings impassable was a dominant feature of borderland life. Security forces blocked minor roads and destroyed bridges to forestall paramilitary movement. Armed checkpoints were installed on main roads, watchtowers dominated, and helicopters patrolled the sky the length of the border. At one stage the Northern Ireland border was the most militarised and surveilled area in Western Europe. Today, this physical infrastructure is almost invisible; the checkpoints have disappeared and there are no more watchtowers. But here and there you will still encounter traces of a troubled past.

At Aghalane I pass beneath one such reminder: the remains of an old bridge and its new replacement. All that exists of the original stone bridge are its steep stone ramparts, austere walls facing each other on opposite sides of the river. It was built in the nineteenth century, with a three-arch span high above the water. When the Troubles intensified, the big old bridge was identified as a potential escape route for the IRA fleeing south over the border. Counter-paramilitaries detonated a bomb beneath it in 1972, severing this key cross-border route. A hasty attempt was made to patch up the damaged structure, but no sooner were repairs complete than it was blown up again, and the crossing remained impassable for many years. The Good Friday Agreement inspired efforts towards peace and reconciliation. What better expression of this than the building of bridges, a physical and moral statement of rapprochement. In 1999 a new bridge was unveiled at Aghalane; the 'Peace Bridge', as it is now called, runs parallel to the original crossing. Its full title is the 'Senator George Mitchell Peace Bridge', in recognition of the US senator's role in brokering the Irish Peace Process talks. The Peace Bridge may not be a thing of beauty, but, judging by the heavy volume of traffic, it is serving as an important social and economic link between communities north and south of the river. While there are no longer any checkpoints, this frontier continues to be a subject of debate and controversy in the wake of Brexit.

As I push farther upstream, the scenery around the river begins to change. Alder, oak, ash and sallies tower overhead, their lower branches catching and vibrating in the strong river flow. They obscure my view of the outside world, but for the time being I welcome the shelter they afford from the rain showers breezing through. The banks have closed in, and are quite steep; there could be problems if I need to leave the river in a hurry.

It's the perfect habitat for kingfishers, and they are abundant here. Blips of electric blue streak ahead of the canoe. I stop counting the sightings after a while. Cruiser boats, heading for the Erne, sweep downstream. The first few encounters are intimidating and I deal with them in my usual overzealous way, but I soon figure out how to navigate through without floundering or getting tangled up in trees. My main concern is ensuring that the pilots see me in time to throttle back their engines. Most are obliging, but a few are oblivious of the vulnerability of an open canoe.

The first lock looms at Corraquill, a steep barrier that I will have to portage the canoe around. Below the lock gates there's a low pontoon where canoes can egress. I climb ashore, carry the canoe and its cargo past the lock chamber, and relaunch on the river's upper level. The process is extremely arduous. Because I'm so concerned about the canoe – God forbid I should get a scratch on the paintwork – I'm overly cautious when it comes to handling it out of the water. If it were made of tough plastic, I would probably be less diligent. My heart sinks at the thought of going through the process at another fifteen locks. The plan had been to overcome at least five locks each day, but it's unlikely I'll achieve this goal. Today, I'll be happy with just two locks and settle for an early night near Ballyconnell, across the border in County Cavan.

Back in the nineteenth century, when it was decided to link the Shannon and the Erne, the engineers chose to work with the existing waterways, rather than building an entire canal from scratch. The result is a combination of two natural rivers, and a scattering of loughs, all interlinked with sections of artificial canal. Hopes were high that the waterway would be busy with goods and passenger traffic. The lifespan of the waterway, in terms of practical use, was very brief, though, because, by the time the navigation was finished, road and rail already had the advantage. Over the course of nine years, fewer than ten boats had travelled its length. For more than a hundred years the waterway lay disused and forgotten. The river and lake sections survived, but the locks collapsed and the still-water canals became clogged and overgrown. Restoration work began in 1991, another symbolic north/south initiative. British and Irish governments pooled resources, and with the help of EU grants and US funding, the route was reopened. The revamped waterway features electronically operated locks,

weirs and several fully serviced marinas. Nowadays, an average of a thousand boats travel along it each year.

Overnight I have revised my timetable; the locks are a serious setback. No doubt they would be manageable with a second pair of helping hands. The aim today is to tackle another two locks, cross the county border into Leitrim and arrive at Aghoo, some twenty kilometres upstream. The rain sets in just as I am packing up camp. It is definitely rain this time, steady and persistent. I pull on waterproofs and paddle stoically upriver. Some time later, the rain eases, the sky clears and the countryside reveals itself. The river is now winding through a seemingly deserted landscape, devoid of roads, villages, buildings, people and livestock, a forgotten world it seems. Ancient texts refer to it as part of *Magh Slécht*, the 'Plain of Prostration'. The origins of the name hark back to the time of Érimón and the legendary pagan god Crom Cruach, a sinister, cult-like figure who held sway over the inhabitants of Cavan. In these parts he is sometimes referred to as 'the bent one on the hill' or 'the crouching darkness'. His likeness is described as a gold idol, surrounded by twelve standing stones. Subjects were forced to kneel in reverence to the idol. It is said that, on threat of withered crops and dry cows, the dark lord demanded the first-born child of each family as human sacrifice; those who failed to comply had their heads dashed against the stones. It took the intervention of St Patrick to release the terrorised people from such a dark and malignant reign. The legend goes on to describe how the fearless saint came travelling along the river in search of the gold idol, whom he struck with a mighty blow of his crozier. As the broken figure came crashing down, a demon sprang up and appeared to St Patrick, who cursed it and cast it into hell. In so doing, he freed the land of pagan beliefs.

This morning's journey has been gruelling, an uphill battle that has me hunched low in the canoe fighting into wind and current. A long slog across a chain of loughs brings me to the shelter of Haughton's Shore at the bottom of Lough Garadice. It's such a relief to limp into the friendly little harbour, flop ashore and stretch cramped muscles.

Aghoo, which I would like to reach by evening, isn't too far away. To get to it, all I have to do is cross the lough. Easier said than done! By early afternoon, squalls are ripping right down the middle of the lough, whipping the water into a frenzy of galloping white horses. As soon as the bow of the canoe pokes past the harbour entrance, a gale-force wind almost flips it over. I retreat behind the harbour wall, surprised and slightly terrified. The opposite shore appears to be more sheltered, but just to get there would be too risky a task. By keeping close to the lakeshore, there might be a chance of making it to the top of the lough. With all the cargo stowed in the bow, I leave the harbour and battle into wind and waves. After a half-hour's punishing work I haven't achieved anything; I'm just paddling on the spot. Breaking waves slosh over the bow and spill into the canoe. The water inside is a rising concern, and there's no time to stop and bail. My energy and confidence start to ebb. I'm way out of my depth in these conditions, and there's no one around to help if things take a nasty turn. The only sensible option is to get off the water and wait for the weather front to pass. In a wide trough between two breaking waves, I turn tail and run back to Haughton's Shore.

The Irish language has many words for rain, each expressing a different type of rainfall. *Fliuch* is an old word that describes a 'wetting' rain, at the upper end of the scale. *Brádán* describes a light, misty rain. On the Shannon–Erne

I've experienced every sort of rain: soft, spitting, drizzle, squib, torrential, pelting, lashing, driving, bucketing, 'rain that would go through a board of oak' and 'raining knives and forks'. But mostly it's been *fliuch*, a steady wetting rain. *But mostly it's been fliuch, a steady wetting rain.'*

Extreme weather was a source of much anxiety in early and medieval times. Livestock and harvests depended on clement weather, and for this the ruling king or chieftain was held liable. The *Annals of the Four Masters* notes an abundance of rain and the failure of crops in the year 975. Writing in the Middle Ages, Gerald of Wales remarked on Ireland's 'plentiful supply of rain, such as ever-present overhanging cloud and fog, that you can scarcely see even in summer three consecutive days of really fine weather'. Wetting rain is not unusual, particularly in these parts of Connacht. The year 1816 is remembered as having been 'without a summer'. The following year, 1817, was described as 'the year of the malty flour'. A third successive year of persistent rainfall led to yet another failed harvest, pushing people to the brink and forcing many to emigrate.

Not far from Haughton's Shore lived the Gaffney family, who, by the end of 1818 found themselves destitute and starving on their small farm holding. Theirs is a familiar tale shared by millions of poverty-stricken Irish who were left with no choice but to leave the country. Things took an unusual turn for the Gaffneys, though, when they set foot on American soil. The heroine of the story is Margaret, the Gaffney family's daughter, who was just five years old when she left the family home for good with her parents.

Their high seas journey was a punishing experience, as the ship they sailed on headed into a series of relentless storms. All passenger luggage was swept overboard, and provisions ran so dangerously low that meals were rationed to one biscuit a day. Six months later the ship limped into Baltimore, Maryland. The Gaffneys were not long settled when a bout of yellow fever ripped through the city, claiming the lives of Margaret's parents, leaving her orphaned and homeless at the age of nine. Against the odds, the tenacious child managed to survive, finding work as a peddler and then as a servant girl. She later married Charles Haughery, a fellow Irish immigrant. Because her husband suffered from poor health, the couple moved to New Orleans, in the hope that warmer climes would be of benefit, but misfortune tailed them. In the 'City of Fever and Fortune', 'Port of Pestilence and Prosperity', who can tell how the dice will fall? Shortly after their move, death claimed both Charles and, within months, Margaret's first-born. Widowed, impoverished and bereft, somehow Margaret found the will to carry on. Out of nothing she created a successful business empire. It started with the purchase of two cows, which Margaret grew to a herd of forty, the foundations of a profitable dairy enterprise. Next came property investments, which saw her assets and wealth increase, followed by her most ambitious and successful enterprise, a bakery – the first steam-powered bakery in the United States, and the largest one at that. With each turn of profit, Margaret ploughed her fortunes back into the community, building orphanages and homeless shelters, supporting charities and distributing milk and bread to the poor and hungry throughout the city. In New

Orleans she is remembered as the 'Angel of the Delta', the 'Mother of the Orphans' or, simply, the 'Bread Woman'. Margaret Haughery is distinguished as being the second woman in the United States to have a statue erected in her honour. Not bad for a woman who couldn't read or write and owned just two dresses at a time.

The rain does not let up over Lough Garadice. The wind has eased but it's still damp, grey and drizzly. Margaret's story should put an end to my whinging; it should lift my spirits, but it hasn't. All my clothes and camping gear are either damp or sodden, which exacerbates the feeling of wretchedness. I had hoped to explore the islands in the area (there are crannogs and castle ruins out in the middle of the lough), but the weather has put paid to those plans. Battling my way to the top of the lough, I rejoin the river, where at least there is some shelter in the narrow, tree-lined channel. Several days of rainfall has made the current stronger. With everything so slick and slippery, it takes double the effort to portage the canoe around locks. I like to think of myself as more than just a fair-weather paddler, but the last few days have been mostly miserable. Thoughts of quitting bubble to the surface.

Every animal, apart from ducks, has gone into hiding, it seems. The impression is of a saturated landscape, dripping, pooling and boggy. Because of the damp climate and water-laden soil, there is little sign of intense or heavy agriculture on the hinterland. There are those who will tell you that land in County Leitrim is sold by the gallon, as opposed to the hectare. You could interpret the countryside as poor and undeveloped, but even through the veil of rain, I can see how rarefied it is. Beyond the riverbank are rough meadows, often brimming with wildflowers. The grass isn't the nitrogen-enriched green I'm accustomed to down south; here, it is tall, spiky and tufted, interspersed with white drifts of angelica and meadowsweet. There's a great diversity of plant life. Sometimes, when I pull into the bank for a toilet break, I find myself in a field full of orchids, such as common, bee and the deep pink of the pyramidal. There's self-heal, red clover, purple loosestrife, thistle and yarrow. Yellow flag irises are profuse along the banks.

Flax was a crop commonly grown in these parts. The fibres of the plant's stems were spun into linen. Flax produces beautiful tiny blue flowers, so the fields around here must have looked unearthly, a glorious azure blue like a clear and cloudless summer sky. It's an ancient crop, cultivated as far back as 1000 BC. In the eighteenth and nineteenth centuries, flax was one of Ireland's chief yields, with linen accounting for half the country's exports. To this day, flax is an emblem of Northern Ireland. Smallholdings were incentivised to grow more and more of it, with spinning wheels awarded to households based on the number of acres planted. A single acre entitled the grower to four spinning wheels. According to the 'Spinning Wheel List' produced by the Irish Linen Board in 1796, there were over 1,700 families in Leitrim growing and spinning flax. It was very much a cottage industry, and was extremely labour-intensive, with all the family members recruited to help. When ready to harvest, the plant was pulled by hand rather than cut at the base. The stalks were left on the ground to dry out, until they turned the colour of straw. Threshing removed the seeds, leaving only the strong fibrous stems. At that point the material would be graded for use as either lace, damask or fine Irish linen. The fibres were then soaked in water to break down enzymes, a process called 'retting', preparing the product for spinning. This job exclusively occupied female members of households. The yarn was then passed on to the linen mills.

The seeds of the plant are also valuable; linseed oil is derived from crushed flax seeds. It's a substance that has a myriad of uses, and for a time was the main ingredient used to waterproof clothing. Worn-out sailcloth, usually linen, was painted with a mixture of linseed oil and wax and sewn into waterproof clothing for sailors and fishermen, giving rise to the term 'oilskin'. The combination of golden-hued linseed oil and wax gave the garments a distinctive yellow colour.

Because of the weather, the subject of waterproof clothing occupies a considerable amount of my head space. My foul-weather gear is made from synthetic fabric and, so far, is doing an excellent job of keeping moisture in as opposed to out! Since so much physical effort goes into paddling, heat and sweat are inevitable. In spite of pulling on the plastic trousers and zipping up my coat every morning, I end the day feeling wetter than if I had just worn a T-shirt and shorts.

The watershed of the Shannon–Erne is at Castlefore, and from here on it is downhill, downstream, all the way to the River Shannon. The rain is still bucketing down. The sky remains overcast and leaden; I haven't seen a hint of blue, let alone the sun, for these past days, and as a result I'm in a ratty mood, short-tempered and bitchy. A man in a white van watches as I haul the canoe out of the river. At this stage I'm used to curious onlookers – also known as gongoozlers – and carry on about my business. As I wheel the canoe past the van, the electric window on the driver's side whirrs open. Despite not having spoken to a single solitary person over the past few days, I have no desire to engage in conversation, and keep walking. A man's voice calls after me.

'Excuse me, sorry, sorry, but I can't help wondering if you intend heading out on the water?'

'Yes. That's the plan.' Gritted teeth, short fuse, don't bother making eye contact.

'Ah, please tell me you're not going to go!'

I stop, turn and look at the man, thrown by his pleading tone.

'Sorry,' he apologises again, 'but I'm the lock keeper, and I'll feel responsible for you if you go out in that.'

I immediately relax, always happy to meet a Waterways Ireland employee. Gerry, it turns out, manages several locks along the River Shannon and the Shannon–Erne Waterway. I explain my journey and try to reassure him that I'm well prepared, showing off my safety gear, life jacket, dry bags and maps. This seems to mollify him somewhat. We exchange phone numbers, and before I move on he says he'll keep an eye out for me at various points along the way. Of course, he would prefer it if I didn't go out at all, but it's touching and comforting to think that someone will be watching out for me.

Then again, Gerry may have had other reasons to be so concerned about me continuing. The stretch of water ahead goes by the name of Lough Marrave, the 'Lake of

Death'. The lough has been festering away at the back of my mind since I started researching this waterway, but the etymology of its name remains a mystery. Some say it may have been a place of sacrificial worship, while others suggest that fish, for some inexplicable reason, are unable to survive in its waters. Myths and folklore are cunning conceits. They lure us in and, despite our best judgement, play tricks with our mind. Hovering at the entrance to the lough as I assess how to best navigate across, a voice inside my head whispers over and over, 'Lake of Death', 'Lake of Death'. It's only a small lough, about a hundred metres from end to end. There's a strong headwind funnelling straight down the centre, together with a fine, billowing mist. Oddly though, the surface is calm, barely a ripple; the wind seems to flatten instead of agitate, which serves only to heighten the aura of mystery. At the far end is Keshcarrigan, a village with a marina, slipway, shelter and drinking water – all incentives to paddle on. *Minnow* skitters crab-like across the lough, taunted by the frisky breeze. Minutes later I bounce the hull up onto the slipway, heart hammering in my chest and breathing turned shallow.

'Myths and folklore are cunning conceits. They lure us in and, despite our best judgement, play tricks with our mind.'

When this stretch of water was being prepared for navigation, an ancient artefact was dredged from the mud. The small, understated object turned out to be a bronze drinking cup dating to the early first century AD. Dubbed

- 95 -

the Keshcarrigan Bowl, it was scrupulously cleaned and analysed before being mounted for exhibition at the National Museum in Dublin. Under artificial light and sheathed in a transparent box, the bowl (or cup – the interpretation is loose) glows, deep, warm and golden. Why the piece was lying in the depths remains a mystery. Was it a votive offering to a Celtic deity? Maybe it was deliberately hidden from thieves and raiders, or perhaps someone simply dropped it there accidentally? Is it a coincidence that it was found near the Lake of Death?

Humans were present here over 3,000 years ago, an ancient race of lake dwellers who changed the waterscape when they decided to build crannogs in the middle of the loughs. Trees were felled and the trunks and branches were stacked, layered and interwoven to create artificial island refuges. Back then, the lake and hinterland would have catered for all primary needs: fresh water, firewood, security, shelter, food. Archaeologists, sifting through the lake dwellers' detritus, have revealed a bounty of artefacts tracing back to the late Stone Age – quern stones, dugout canoes, axe heads, weapons, charred animal bones and moulds for casting copper and bronze. The lake retreats are wild and shaggy now, almost impossible to penetrate and explore. Their shallow shorelines are tricky places to navigate, as I soon discover when I paddle in close. Just beneath the canoe is a forest of jagged, black tree stumps. The motorboats are directed well clear of these places and, despite the shallow displacement of my canoe, even I am obliged to retreat. Skirting around the islands' leeward shores, I guide the canoe through dense thickets of willows that slowly colonise the lough.

There are friendlier shores at Prison Island, where I beach the canoe and get out to stretch my cramped legs. The island was the site of a notorious jail in the seventeenth and eighteenth centuries, a place where hangings and beheadings were a regular event, and where prisoners were subjected to inhuman conditions. Sitting on the cells' crumbled ramparts, I finish off the last of my cheese – rind end, rubbery and tasteless. It's a miserable place to bide the time, and all the more so when my mood is already at such a low ebb.

At the top of the lough, I give way to a bevy of swans being herded along by an oncoming barge steaming up the channel. As soon as the birds reach the lough's open water, they take to the air, their huge webbed feet treading the surface until they achieve lift-off, wings beating noisily and energetically. Waiting for the barge to emerge, I throw a last glance over the landscape. Lough Scur, 'Lake of the Horses', is a placid yet mysterious place. There is no sign of any horses, but I recognise, parked on the verge on the crest of a hill, a white van, and a man standing by it, peering through binoculars. Gerry, true to his word, is watching out for me. He can head home now and sleep soundly, knowing I have safely made it this far.

For a considerable distance the canal cuts through a gorge of solid rock. Sheer walls rise up on either side, dripping wet and alive with tenacious ferns and wild flowers. Swallows soar and skim the waters ahead, their chirruping calls echoing off the passage walls. Travelling along this corridor implies a sense of impending departure, of transitioning from one world to another.

The end of the waterway is almost in sight. This should lift my mood, but it doesn't change the way I feel.

Knicker elastic has sawn a wound across my hip bone.
It stings like hell with every pull and twist of the paddle.
There's a permanent drip attached to the end of my nose,
and my stomach complains incessantly with hunger. At the
end of the channel, Kilclare lock swims into focus. Beyond

it is a flight of seven locks that will drop the water level down through Leitrim village and into the River Shannon. Either I take on the locks individually, relaunching after each one and paddling the short distance in between, or I haul the canoe and cargo in one go along the bank for five kilometres. Both options defeat me. Sitting on the dock, unable to summon any more energy, I decide to finish the journey right here for the time being. No more locks. No more camping. No more *fliuch*. A friend has a house in the neighbourhood, and it's there I find shelter until the weather and my mood improve.

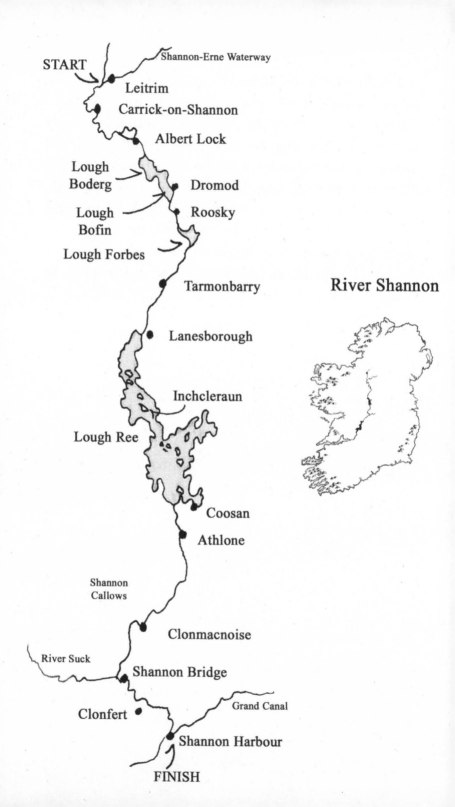

START

Shannon-Erne Waterway

Leitrim

Carrick-on-Shannon

Albert Lock

Lough Boderg

Dromod

Lough Bofin

Roosky

Lough Forbes

Tarmonbarry

Lanesborough

Inchcleraun

Lough Ree

Coosan

Athlone

Shannon Callows

Clonmacnoise

River Suck

Shannon Bridge

Clonfert

Grand Canal

Shannon Harbour

FINISH

River Shannon

River Shannon

The water is deceptively calm in the shelter of the harbour. It lulls me into a false sense of security and optimism, so that I am taken off guard by what lurks around the corner. The Shannon is hidden by a curtain of tall reeds, waiting and ready to pounce. Launching its attack, it snatches hold of my canoe, tossing, mauling and shaking it from bow to stern. I back paddle and flail about helplessly midstream, trying desperately to scramble back to the safety of the harbour, but it's too late. The river has me firmly in its grips, stunned and terrified; there's nothing I can do but surrender to the flow.

The rain had eased somewhat when I launched the canoe in Leitrim village to start my descent of the Shannon. At least the persistent deluge has been replaced by sporadic downpours, punctuated with bright, sunny intervals. It's about as good as it gets in this part of the country. The marina was a hive of activity, with a steady stream of boats heading up and down the Shannon–Erne Waterway, while others popped in from the River Shannon junction. During a lull in the traffic and rain, I had pushed away from the jetty and paddled straight into the lion's den.

The Shannon boils and seethes. The water runs a murky grey-brown, with dirty blobs of foam eddying around the surface. With the best possible will, I try to navigate the surging water, though I'm not entirely sure how to do so. There is really no need to paddle; I just steer and keep *Minnow*'s bow pointing downstream – no matter what. It will be 'curtains' if the canoe turns broadside to the flow. The banks whizz by so fast that I register no details. Mostly, there are no banks – the floodwater is so high that the river has spilled into the fields on either side. When the canoe skims over a fence post, I know I may be in trouble. Now the river races over grassland, and I briefly lose track of the main boating channel. The next few bends pass in a blur as I veer around trees, swerve past navigation markers and dodge flotsam. My only hope is that this roller-coaster ride will ease a little farther downstream; until then I am the mouse in the cat's claws, the rabbit in the fox's jaws, destined to be swallowed whole.

'There is really no need to paddle; I just steer and keep Minnow's bow pointing downstream – no matter what.'

Accurately pinpointing the source of a river satisfies our rational minds, though it is rarely possible to identify a single point of origin since most rivers arise from a meeting of multiple streams. Mythical stories of their creation are a familiar thread running through ancient civilisations. The mythical source of the River Shannon is said to be Connla's Well, 'The Well of Wisdom', which is fringed by nine hazel trees. These trees bear magical fruits, which drop into the deep well and are consumed by a salmon that swims there in the darkness – the Salmon of Knowledge. Those who drink from the well or eat the fish will be rewarded with wisdom and inspiration. Sionnan, granddaughter of Lir, the Celtic God of the Sea, took it upon herself to seek out this fountain of knowledge, despite having been warned not to do so. As she approached the well, the salmon reacted forcefully, stirring up the water so that it overflowed, drowning Sionnan and carrying her body out to sea. It is from this legend that the river is believed to have been named.

The source of the Shannon can be traced high up in the Cuilcagh hills that straddle the border between counties Cavan and Fermanagh. It so happened that the area was not far from where I had been sheltering at my friend's house in Leitrim. I had to investigate. The lonely hills are alive with streams, each one competing for the title of the river's original source. The Shannon Pot is a dark well of unfathomable depth that bubbles energetically in the corner of a wild-flower meadow. An appealing air of mystery cloaks the site, and it is easy to see how some believe it to be the legendary Connla's Well. It is surrounded by willows of some kind and, yes, there is even a hazelnut tree. The overflow gurgles away down the hillside and spills into Lough Allen, the first of the Shannon's many broad lakes. Gathering pace, the youthful river sweeps past Leitrim village and flows through the countryside until it reaches the Atlantic Ocean on the country's west coast. At 360 kilometres, the Shannon is Ireland's longest river.

Superlatives abound when it comes to describing the River Shannon. It is mighty, majestic, splendid, glorious and noble, words more familiarly associated with rivers such as the Amazon, Nile or Mississippi. As a solo voyager in a tiny canoe, I make a point of ignoring the hyperbole. Besides, I don't intend to travel the entire length of the river, only around a third of it.

Somehow, I manage to hold my nerve on the turbulent ride downriver. It is a huge relief to skid up onto the slipway at Carrick-on-Shannon, and stand on solid ground, knees knocking and breathless. Wandering the streets of Carrick gives me time to decompress, and I have a chance encounter with a memorial stone that excites my interest. The memorial celebrates the life of Susan Langstaff Mitchell, 'poet and mystic of the Irish Cultural Renaissance', who was born in Carrick in 1866. Included on the stone is her ode to Carrick:

> I will not walk these roads of pain,
> I will turn back to youth again,
> 'Tis full sunlight, though passed the noon,
> The night will not come very soon,
> And if we haste we may lie down,
> Before sunset in Carrick Town.

Mitchell's name and legacy were unknown to me until now. A casual browse online reveals a striking redhead with flawless pale skin and sad brown eyes. Her portrait is in the collection of the National Gallery of Ireland and was painted by John Butler Yeats, father of William Butler Yeats and Jack B. Yeats. The young Susan Mitchell looks stunning, a Titian beauty who started out life on the banks of the Shannon and went on to carve out a career as a writer and satirist, the latter accomplishment earning her the moniker 'red-headed rebel'.

Susan was born into a Protestant family, and her father was the manager of the Provincial Bank of Ireland in Carrick. Following her father's untimely death, her mother, facing financial hardship, sent Susan off to be raised by relatives in Dublin and Birr. Her familial connections brought her into contact with the figureheads of Ireland's cultural renaissance, including the Yeats family, the Purser family, Constance Markievicz and Lady Gregory. Having graduated from Trinity College in Dublin, Susan describes her years of early adulthood as like 'a cork on a wave'. During those blossoming years she developed tuberculosis, and was obliged to travel for treatment to London, where she stayed as a guest of the Yeats family. It was in London that she discovered her calling:

> Always the talk turned back to Ireland and it seemed to me that in this London suburb I saw Ireland truly for the first time; as one cannot see oneself in a mirror by pressing one's nose against the glass, I had to leave my country to find her.

The Irish cultural renaissance saw a flourishing of creative talent – poetry, music, art, literature and plays – that gathered momentum in the late nineteenth century. The movement coincided with an upsurge in political nationalism, and a driving force behind it was W.B. Yeats.

Returning to Ireland, Susan determined to establish

herself as a writer, securing work as sub-editor of the *Irish Homestead*. Under the pseudonym 'Brighid', she wrote a column entitled 'Household Hints'. More than simply 'how to' advice with domestic chores, the platform was an outlet for her to discuss issues of gender equality and the Irish cultural revival. Living in Dublin, Susan moved in the select echelons of the capital's literary and artistic circles, mixing with the likes of George Bernard Shaw, Oliver St John Gogarty and the artists Paul Henry and Sarah Purser. Susan hosted salons at her home, evenings of poetry recitals, music and literary discussions. Guests were like-minded company with whom she shared an interest in expressions of Irish culture.

Susan worked for many years as a literary critic, contributing book reviews to the *Irish Times* and articles to the *Irish Statesman* and *The Freeman's Journal*. Her writing style is noted as quick-witted and satirical. She could sing too, and she used the gift as a platform for political lampooning. A book of her ballads bears the title *Aids to the Immortality of Certain Persons in Ireland*. Later she joined Sinn Féin and wrote for that party's newspaper. She was involved in the formation of the United Irishwomen, an organisation committed to improving social and educational opportunities for women. Her health was dogged by tuberculosis and she became progressively deaf. Although she lived and died in Dublin, she never forgot her Carrick roots, and her memories of the River Shannon were wistful and romantic. Her lifelong friend George Russell (Æ) described her as 'one of the best Irishwomen of her time'.

It is well past noon, and I need to keep moving downstream. There's another ten kilometres of this wild water ahead, which should bring me to Jamestown. The Blueways kayaking guide estimates a journey time of three hours, so I should arrive there just in time to pitch the tent before sunset. At the foot of the slipway the river lies in wait, taunting and tugging at *Minnow*'s keel as soon as it touches water. I climb into the hull and brace myself for round two. At least this time I won't be caught off guard.

Rivers are powerful adversaries. They can be your enemy and your undoing. A small open canoe is unequally matched against such a powerful opponent. The only weapon at my disposal is a twin-blade paddle. It is made of wood and is a beautifully crafted object in its own right. The paddle has the added advantage of having a two-part adjustable shaft. By adjusting the ferrule joint, the blades can be set in two different positions, feathered or parallel. Generally, I keep the blades feathered, so that they are at right angles to each other. As one blade moves through the water, the opposite side slices through the air, reducing wind resistance. Feathered blades place a heavy workload on the wrists, which are constantly in motion. Before leaving Carrick, I reposition the blades so that they are parallel, mirroring each other on either side – this limits the stroke of the paddle, but increases the breaking action. Given the still strong current, I decided that I wouldn't need much forward propulsion, just a means of steering.

'Rivers are powerful adversaries. They can be your enemy and your undoing.'

The river surges on, and with it goes the canoe, bobbing about like Susan Mitchell's proverbial 'cork on a wave'. I flash past ritzy marinas, where row upon row of floating pontoons are filled with luxury private and chartered hire boats. There's a whiff of the French Riviera about it all. The vernacular Shannon boat is plastic-hulled and painted ubiquitous white with go-faster stripes. Each multi-storey vessel has tinted windows, and many are kitted out with swimming platforms. All are equipped with steering wheels, bow and stern thrusters and even windscreen wipers. If there is a traditional Shannon boat, I have yet to see one, though it's good to see the river being used and being important to local economies.

The river hurries on, curling in a tight bow around the town, then racing eastwards, bracing sharply south, west and back east again. In these upper reaches, the river is erratic and confused as it figures out the optimum route down to the waiting sea. Below Carrick the river spills into Lough Corry, where it has a chance to simmer down and relax its hold on the canoe. The water is suddenly submissive and I am briefly back in control, able to dictate pace and direction. The waterscape is littered with foam, mini bergs of dirty polystyrene that tumble and scud about. Leaving the lough, the river pinches in again, but is still puzzling out which way to run. Now it doubles back, heading north-east, in the opposite direction. It feels as if I am on a wild goose chase through the countryside.

It's at this point that engineers and navigators decided to take matters into their own hands, building a canal and bypassing surplus lengths of coiled and shoaly river. The Jamestown Canal is a short stretch of artificial waterway, incorporating a lock on its lower reaches. It's a big relief to exit the river and enter the tame, stationary waters of the canal. Albert Lock is not listed on the Blueways guide as a designated camping ground, but it appeals to me because it is well off the beaten track and away from curious onlookers.

I rise bright and early to find that the weather has, at last, turned in my favour, and I will have a strong following wind to help me on my journey. I stow the bulk of my camping gear in the canoe's stern. This lifts the bow high out of the water, helping the canoe track straight downwind, a simple trick that will save me valuable paddling energy. The gusty wind and strong current ferry the canoe effortlessly downstream, depositing me at the entrance of Lough Boderg. River traffic is confined to a channel running down the centre of the lough since the shores are too shallow for most vessels. Hugging Boderg's rocky eastern shoreline, the canoe runs fast, cresting and surfing the waves. It's a joyous and exhilarating ride once I overcome an initial fear of broaching and capsizing. The canoe takes the pacey conditions in her stride, and I'm impressed with her performance, even though she is designed for flat-water paddling. Within an hour I reach the far end of the lough, where the shores converge to form a narrow pinch-point as the river flows into Lough Bofin. The sheer volume of water squeezing through the tight gap creates a powerful current. Boats heading upstream struggle against the flow, and when I arrive there's a bottleneck of vessels waiting to pass through. Even with engines running at full throttle, their progress is painfully slow. Anchoring the canoe in a reed bed, I sit back and watch the activity unfold. When the coast is clear, I let the current whisk me through and out into Lough Bofin.

Setting out across Bofin, it is as though I have passed into a different world. Where Boderg was vigorous and rushing, Bofin is slumbering, silent and eerily still. The white-knuckle ride ends abruptly, and I am back to self-propulsion again. The shoreline is full of shallow recesses that are off limits to the average boat. Relaxed and unhurried, I dip in and out of coves to explore hidden inlets.

Every lough seems to have its own Rabbit Island. Bofin's sits at the tip of a long finger of land jutting into the lough. The approaches are dangerously shallow and strewn with jagged rocks. If the water was any way choppy, it would be impossible to navigate. There's something about its hostile frontage that draws me closer to its shores. With the canoe tied to an overhanging tree, I step out in ankle-deep water and walk ashore. The interior of the island appears impenetrable. Stunted trees form a shield that daylight is unable to pierce. The ground is solid rock, with hardly a blade of grass or any greenery. How have the trees taken root? Blackthorn slashes into skin and hooks at my hair; struggling and tugging only makes matters worse. Soon I am engrossed with untangling and extricating myself from the clutching thorns. There's a hint of the Brothers Grimm's *Thorn Rose* about the place, as though I have stumbled into a fairy tale where the wood features as a metaphorical boundary between defeat and success. The allusion plays havoc with my mind. Unease threatens to spill over into panic as I turn back and stumble out of the dark and tangled forest. My sandalled feet feel cold, wet and slippery. Looking down, I see they are covered in frogs. The ground is teeming with them, dark brown and no bigger than my little toe. I can't move but for standing on them. It's so surreal and freakish that I scramble back into the canoe to escape them. Rabbit

Island, I decide, is a savage place. I never imagined that I would encounter such a strange part of the world. Having nothing of value for humans, it can't be developed for real estate or agriculture, and has been left to its own devices. The natural world has taken over in its own unique way.

I leave the island and drift downriver, stopping every so often to watch great crested grebes hunt in the shallows. A speedboat streaks by at hair-raising speed. Twin engines, each 150 horsepower, thrust the vessel's bow high into the air. The grebes dive for cover, never to be seen again. The hinterland is defined by sheltering woodland, gently sloping hills and lush green pastures, where muscular bullocks lead charmed lives languishing in enriched fields. I pull into Dromod's small, neat harbour, which is busy with chartered holiday boats, but not overly crowded. As the evening fades, I pitch the tent in a quiet corner and sleep deeply.

Below Dromod the banks of the Shannon close in again and the river eases its pace; from this point its course is less meandering. Today's paddle will be a long and steady one. The aim is to reach Lough Ree, twenty-five kilometres downstream. With the current on my side I should reach it within five hours, but with two locks to portage the canoe around, progress may be slowed. The first lock is at Roosky, which I reach in the early morning. After a relatively easy exit and relaunch, a straight run takes me

through Lough Forbes and down to Tarmonbarry lock, where the portage is a bit more tricky – or maybe I'm starting to tire. A last push brings me to Lanesborough and the top of Lough Ree.

For much of the day's journey I am alone on the river, shrouded from the outside world by high banks of tawny reeds. The rhythm of the paddle induces a state of reverie. When wind and current are in my favour, canoeing is easy work, and I believe I can paddle on forever. With each effortless stroke, the paddle blades rotate at a steady, hypnotic pace, and the riverbanks slip by quietly and slowly. On these rare days of measured progress I am liberated from the oppressive weight of anxieties and indecision, and can feel a subtle revitalising of mind and body taking place.

One of my kayaking inspirations is Audrey Sutherland, an American solo adventurer. Her chosen mode of transport was an inflatable canoe, and she preferred to travel alone. In her lifetime she paddled over 19,000 kilometres, the equivalent of half a circumnavigation of the earth. Audrey's travel adventures spanned five decades, but it wasn't until she was into her sixties that she began exploring Alaska and British Columbia, her example demonstrating that age and gender are not obstacles to exploration. She was still heading off on expeditions well into her eighties. Her early adventures were centred on the islands of Hawaii, where she would set off on long-distance swimming expeditions, her camping gear, including wine, wrapped up in a shower curtain and towed behind her. She graduated on to an inflatable kayak, using it to explore thousands of kilometres of waterways in North America and Europe, even squeezing in a few rivers and lakes in Ireland. Audrey travelled on a shoestring – no sponsors, no camera crews and no social media. Thankfully, she did write up her adventures, and had several books published. *Paddling North* recounts her

'Like the other wild creatures around me, I wake early, a sixth sense propelling me from my warm earthen nest.'

1,300-kilometre solo journey along the Alaskan coast. Her descriptions of the wilderness are rich and vivid, while the practical aspects of the challenge are surprisingly matter-of-fact. She was a knowledgeable forager, renowned for her gourmet campfire meals. Audrey's advice to aspiring travellers was: 'go simple, go solo, go now'.

The Shannon Blueway guide ends at Lanesborough, and beyond this point the river empties into the giant reservoir that is Lough Ree. It's getting late, and I need to pull in and find a place to pitch the tent. The shoreline is low-lying, boggy pasture that slides seamlessly beneath the water. There is endless potential here for camping which runs the risk of setting off my 'Goldilocks Syndrome' – too rocky, too scrubby, too exposed, too many livestock, too stoney, too boggy. I'm not really sure what I'm looking for, but I'll know it when I see it. At last, I find the perfect retreat a short distance downstream – close enough to walk

back to Lanesborough for supplies, yet inaccessible to any cars, people and cattle. Tomorrow I should be perfectly positioned to take on Lough Ree.

Like the other wild creatures around me, I wake early, a sixth sense propelling me from my warm earthen nest. The fog comes as quite a surprise when I unzip the tent door shortly after dawn. It was not a factor I had ever considered or even read about, but, then again, the conditions are perfect for it: warm water, cool air. The river smoke is dense, billowing and saturating. Visibility is less than ten metres; I know the river is there – I just can't see it. So much for an early start. Dressed and ready for action, I find myself grounded and forced to stay under canvas.

The veil lifts slowly, revealing a heavy and windless day. I fill the canoe with my belongings and pass a final glance over last night's camp. The flattened grass where I lay curled has already sprung back to life. I push the canoe across the meadow towards the river. The dragging hull and my bare footprints leave deep impressions in the soft, muddy shoreline, like the imprints of some giant tetrapod from Devonian times. I clasp the smooth oak thwart and guide the hull through the shallows in search of clear water. Somewhere in the rushy beds a heron shrieks, waterfowl scatter and lapwings pipe. Lingering clouds of river smoke drift above the lough, thin wisps condensing and dissolving in the warming midsummer air. I slip into the canoe, take up the paddle and dip the blade tips lightly into the peaty water. Swiftly and silently the canoe glides out across the lough in search of Otherworlds.

Lough Ree, 'the Lake of Kings', represents a milestone in my canoe voyage, a halfway point in my *immram*.

Since I first set out along the River Erne, 250 kilometres has slipped beneath *Minnow*'s keel. The lough has a forbidding reputation; its mercurial waters can change from fair to foul in the blink of an eye. Small boats, open ones in particular, can be caught off guard when the lough bares its teeth. An inconvenient wind will conjure steep breaking waves with short troughs in between. Ree has exacted a heavy price down through the years, prompting the Royal National Lifeboat Institution (RNLI) to open a fully equipped and manned lifeboat station at Coosan Point in 2012. It happens to be one of the busiest stations in the country. Warnings duly noted, I have marked a series of possible routes on the navigation chart. The map looks like a spider's web, with colour-coded lines marking out Plans A, B, C and D. Everything will depend on the weather, the wind's strength and direction. I take a deep breath and send the canoe forward.

The upper reaches of this large body of water are becalmed and empty, mine alone to explore. Water and the sky are shades of grey, distinguishable from each other only by a thin dark strip of shoreline. The stillness, silence and wanness is disconcerting, as if all detail has mysteriously evaporated with the fog. I strain to pick out familiar sounds from the human world, but all I hear is the dip and splash of the paddle and my internal monologue. *Minnow*'s bow cuts cleanly through the still water, casting chevron waves out across the mill pond.

The harebells are blooming on Inchcleraun. A magnificent carpet of blue starting at the island's shore stretches deep into its wooded interior. I leap from the canoe and fall to my knees among the blooms, running my fingers through the coarse grass and caressing the flower's delicate blue bonnets. Harebells, harebells, nobody ever mentioned the harebells in all my readings about the island; all they ever wrote about was Maeve, the mythical warrior queen, who lived and died on these shores. While there's simply no side-stepping this legendary female and her association with Inchcleraun, I want to indulge for just a little while in this enchanting garden.

Ancient myths and legends are enthralling bedtime stories, with their casts of fantastical characters, gripping plot lines and happy-ever-after endings. Like many children, I was introduced to these stories from a very young age. The heroes of these tales were always men – strong, handsome warriors, who managed to have all the most exciting adventures. When women featured, they were generally pretty creatures in urgent need of rescue, or wicked shrews who got their just deserts. Of all the Celtic tales in which women feature, Maeve's story stands apart. In a single, deliberate blow, she shatters the universal narrative of the fragile and submissive female.

Having been nurtured on these wondrous ancestral tales, I find that the time has come to confront this heroic woman and examine her enduring appeal. A warrior and a queen, Maeve is depicted as fearless, confident and charismatic. Queen Maeve, *Medb*, 'she who intoxicates', is the type of woman irresistible to men, and for women too she holds a certain sway. She was also deeply flawed, prone to jealousy, a murderer and a warmonger. My own curiosity is tempered and circumspect. Is she simply a mythical creation, or was she a flesh-and-blood person clothed in imaginative detail?

By all accounts she came from a troubled royal dynasty, bound up in a tangled web of incest, infanticide, cannibalism and bloodthirsty murder. Three daughters were born to Eochu Feidlech, High King of Ireland. Clothru, the eldest, slept with each of her triplet brothers and subsequently gave birth to their child. Eithne, who lurks in the background, was reputed to eat the flesh of new babies and small children. Then Maeve, power-hungry and simmering with jealousy, killed her sister Clothru and thus stole the title Queen of Connacht. Maeve relished a good fight and sent her armies into battle over petty disagreements. Her ambition to own the strongest and biggest bull resulted in 'The Cattle Raid of Cooley', a long and bitter war. After six marriages and a string of lovers, the battle-scarred and weary Maeve retired to the seclusion of Inchcleraun, where she lived out her days. Here on these shores where I have beached my canoe, she built herself a palace and walled garden, all traces of which have long since disappeared.

There are ruins to explore on the island, buildings left behind by early Christians who settled on the islands of Lough Ree and established monasteries. A short stumble along a path rutted by cloven hooves leads me to a clearing in the trees. Walls of dark-grey stone are heavily encrusted with lichen – abstract, multi-coloured smears in the drip style of Jackson Pollock. Roofless rooms are colonised by ragwort, brambles and ash sapling. Ivy, moss and ferns sprout out of nooks and crannies. The midday sun burns down, and the humidity climbs to an oppressive level. I stumble over ground that is potholed and puckered, feeling a bit drunk and delirious. What's the opposite of 'sea legs'? *Mal de debarquement*, 'illness of disembarkment', weak-legged from too many days spent on the water. It's probably just the heat. I scramble over a stile and crawl into the corner of a cool, dark vault and wait for my equilibrium to settle. There's a story going round that females are forbidden entry to one of these churches, and those who disobey the rule will die within the year. The trouble is, no one has seen fit to identify which is the accursed building.

What I really need is a long drink of water. On the way back to the canoe, I lose my footing in a jumble of half-buried stones. Rubbing a wounded knee, I notice delicate carvings on the faces of several stones. The markings are extremely subtle, but, even to my amateur eye, the repeated motifs are unmistakably Romanesque. They appear to be cornerstones, perhaps marking an entrance gate or doorway. Grey/brown stones sullied with lime-green accretions of lichen and woolly tufts of moss – so different to the other masonry, these are definitely sandstone, not indigenous. Layers of history have accumulated and are now slowly sinking back into the earth. In the days of warring tribes, putting down roots on a secluded island must have seemed like a common sense ideal. Inchcleraun is not the easiest place to get to – several kilometres of risky waters separate it from the mainland on all sides. There's no deepwater pier or jetty, and its shoreline is shallow and rock-strewn. In spite of these obstacles, the island was invaded and plundered year after year. Records show an exhausting

'Suspended in the velvety deep, I am entranced by the play of golden light shafts in the waters above.'

list of devastating attacks, not only from Vikings but also local and regional warlords. There was always something irresistible about the place, and settlers were determined to eke out a living on Inchcleraun until the mid-twentieth century. Old black-and-white photographs show thatched and whitewashed cottages, cobbled yards and outbuildings. The island is no longer inhabited, though farmers continue to graze livestock there.

Sitting in the shade of an old ash tree down by the shoreline, I come to the realisation that this must be the place referred to as *Grianán Maeva*, 'Maeve's sunny place'. According to the tales, Maeve would make her way down to the shore each morning and bathe. The location is perfectly suited, secreted from the outside world, away from prying eyes. Having come all this way, it would be a shame not to follow in Maeve's footsteps, so I remove my shoes, undress and enter the water.

I wade out through the shallows, picking my way around the stony debris. The ice-cold water nips playfully as it inches up my legs. When it reaches waist level, I sink slowly into its embrace and kick free of solid ground. Striking out into deeper water, I dive down into the depths, exhaling sharply as the water closes in over my head. Visibility is poor. The water is the colour of polished amber, having been stained a deep tannic-brown when it filtered through the boglands. Below me the lough is dark, mysterious and fathomless. Suspended in the velvety deep, I am entranced by the play of golden light shafts in the waters above. Then I slowly let myself rise and break the surface.

Not so long ago women would have been arrested if they were found swimming in lakes and rivers. It was against the law for them to do so until the twentieth century. Swimming was not something women were generally keen to partake in. Aside from being unlawful, another possible reason for their reluctance was its association with 'Trial by Water', the practice of submerging women in water to determine if they were witches. If the woman floated, she was a witch; if she drowned, she wasn't. The last time a woman endured this ordeal was in 1809. By the eighteenth century, women were taking to the water and 'bathing', an activity that took place on segregated beaches within the British Empire. However, they were still banned from swimming in lakes, rivers or ponds, and were arrested for doing so.

An additional challenge women faced was the clothing they were obliged to wear while bathing. They had to be covered from head to toe, and that included wearing stockings and shoes. Since clothes were made of wool, they naturally dragged the body down when waterlogged, making it impossible to swim. The first swimming costumes for women were invented in the early years of the twentieth century, when Annette Kellerman, dubbed the 'Australian Mermaid', pioneered a one-piece suit that exposed only the lower legs.

During the Victorian era sea bathing increased in popularity among women to such an extent that mixed bathing was permitted on some beaches. In Ireland, bylaws were enacted in the late nineteenth century requiring the existence of segregated bathing areas on popular beaches. Any person found in breach of these rules was liable to a penalty not exceeding forty shillings.

The 'swimming suffragettes' were pioneering women who campaigned for equality in swimming. The movement coincided with the suffragette activists, who campaigned for political freedom and sought the vote for women. A pivotal event in the ambitious swimming suffragettes' campaign occurred in April 1914, when the activists advertised a 'Water Carnival' at Hyde Park's Serpentine Lido in London. The women arrived at Hyde Park, paraded around the lake and flung off their wraps, revealing themselves in bathing costumes, each with a letter pinned to their chests. Together the letters spelled out the word S-U-F-F-R-A-G-E. It would be a few more decades before mixed bathing was permitted at the Serpentine. In June 1930 long queues formed outside the lido gates to take part in the first authorised 'mixed bather'. Very slowly it became more acceptable for women to swim everywhere. The British suffrage campaigner Margaret Nevinson is quoted as saying, 'it cost us a long and weary struggle to win, not the freedom of the sea, but the freedom of rivers and lakes and ponds'.

'I can't leave, don't want to leave, but I must leave; the heroes of the voyage tales never stay anywhere for long.'

Ireland was somewhat slower in adapting to these new norms, and certain public swimming spots continued to deny women access. On 20 July 1974, a group of women invaded the Forty Foot in Sandycove, a male-only swimming area, demanding equal access. The women marched in carrying placards bearing slogans such as 'Out from under and into the swim' and 'We'll fight them on the beaches, we'll win between the sheets.' As they changed into bikinis and swimming togs, they were met with a torrent of abuse from their male counterparts. Since the protest, female bathers are now fully accepted at the Forty Foot.

How long have I been lying here among the harebells? I must have dozed off. Time, I'm always obsessed with the time. How long will it take? Do I have enough time to do this, that and the other? It's the one annoying tie that keeps me bound to reality. Inchcleraun has cast a spell. From the moment I stepped ashore, a threshold was crossed. Could this be my Tír na nÓg, a land where time stands still and there is no illness or sorrow? The *immram* tales describe it as an earthy paradise, a forested wilderness with flowery meadows, reached by an enchanted boat, a place where parting is 'sweet as honey' and maybe forever. I can't leave, don't want to leave, but I must leave; the heroes of the voyage tales never stay anywhere for long. I dress and repack my scattered belongings: water bottle, camera, lunch box and apple core – the lens cap of my camera has mysteriously disappeared. As I paddle away from Inchcleraun's shores, something tells me not to look back; that to do so will break the spell.

The waters of Lough Ree are still mercifully calm, and I point *Minnow*'s bow for distant shores. A convoy of cruise boats sails up the main navigation channel. They seem to hunt in packs of threes and fours, and only in the hours either side of lunchtime. The anglers, on the other hand, are out at all hours of the day, revving up their engines in the early-morning hours, putt-putting up and down, over and back, long into the evening.

I set out for Barley Harbour, which, according to the charts, has a pier, slipway and, I hope, some green space to pitch camp. People speak well of the wild camping there. I hear the music long before I reach the harbour. A heavy bass beat pulses out across the open water. Hot on its heels comes the smell of red meat grilling on a barbecue. Something isn't right here. The canoe glides quietly into the harbour wall's embrace. A brief circuit confirms my initial fears: the harbour is home to a tented city; every blade of grass is occupied. Music blasts from car radios, refuse bins overflow, plastic shopping bags bulging with empty beer cans are stacked in a high pyramid. As I approach the slipway, two wiener dogs dressed in matching his and hers life jackets race down to the water's edge and bark dementedly at me. Crowds of onlookers are drawn to the scene. I spin the canoe about and beat a hasty retreat back into the bay.

The experience has left me feeling a bit put out. Whatever spell lingered from Inchcleraun has been well and truly shattered. It's the middle of summer and a long weekend to boot, so the beauty spots are bound to be swamped. I should have known better. If I don't feel like sharing, there's no other option but to travel on and find another patch. The rocky shoreline pushes me farther and farther downstream. By now it's so hot that fish are hurling themselves out of the water. I travel in the company of angling punts, ten to fifteen vessels chugging back and forth along the shore with fishing line trailing astern. At a small inlet three boats are beached ashore. Over an open fire a group of men boil a tea kettle and pan-fry trout. I recognise the fishermen, having passed them several times during the day. We wave and shout hellos over the water. The scent of wood smoke and butter-braised fish is positively mouthwatering, and follows me companionably as I paddle southwards.

I find my own private inlet a little farther on. Someone at some stage has cleared the shallows of stones, exposing a sandy strip perfect for landing boats. The cove is only

a few metres wide, barely enough room for the tent and canoe. Blackthorn thickets with sloe berries swelling on their stems engulf the space. The camping is far from ideal; there's no soil to sink the tent pegs into, just silty mud. I try to dispel covetous thoughts of Barley Harbour and what could have been.

As the morning unfolds, a frisky breeze picks up, puffing out of the south-west and dancing into my tiny cove. Nursing a battered enamel mug of rehydrated foaming latte, I sit and watch the wavelets lap against the shore and chew the inside of my cheek anxiously. Early birds already on the wing are faint scribbles across the brightening sky. The agitated water shimmers and flashes like a gigantic disco ball. It should be manageable, provided the weather holds steady, though the heavy cloud formations do not bode well. I break camp and stow as much cargo as possible in the bow, while still leaving some leg room. Then it's off into the headwind and a long morning paddle, bouncing past the Black Island archipelago, skittering across the wide mouth of Inny Bay to a pit stop in the sheltered waters behind Inchturk and Inchmore.

A surreptitious change has overcome the lakeside. The hard rocky shoreline has yielded to a lush and varied flora – purple loosestrife, yellow flag irises, burr reed and mare's-tail flourish along the margins. The pale-blue faces of water forget-me-nots smile up at me from their semi-submerged habitat. Sorrel, water mint, yellow cress and other wetland herbs form a magical carpet, thriving both underwater and in open air.

Just off the bow is a dazzling white bird with plumage the colour of crisply bleached linen. It paddles knee-deep, its beady eyes earnestly studying the water. It's probably a little egret, but looks more heron-sized. Could it be a great egret? They have been sighted in recent years around the east coast with increasing frequency. This is a busy bird, full of urgent action, tottering about on long spindly legs like a stilt walker at a street carnival. I creep up from behind, as quietly as possible, but the wary bird takes to the air in a fluid swoop and glides away downstream.

Egrets, little and great, were quite a common bird in Ireland up to the late nineteenth century, when the fashion world decided that their dazzling white plumes looked far better on hats than on the birds themselves. One Victorian plume dealer is recorded as having sold two million egret skins. Egrets retreated south, hiding out around the Mediterranean and along the coast of north Africa, where the climate was more pleasant and the risk of being lynched greatly reduced. Gradually the birds started moving north again, up through France, across the channel into England, and then, in 1997, the first of the egrets arrived in County Cork.

The swans are swimming business-like inshore, which is not a good sign. I sidle out of a sheltered bay to investigate the scene. The breeze has escalated into a gusty blow and the water has dulled to a cold and ominous grey. The slightest change in wind speed always feels amplified from the perspective of a canoe. A short run due south will bring me to the end of the lough. There's no time to lose, so I paddle strongly and feel my shoulders burn. By the time I dodge behind Hare Island, I'm bursting for a pee. The island's jetty is distinctly marked as 'PRIVATE' by a hand-painted sign. Out of urgency I ignore it, beach the canoe and thrash about in nettles for a friendly piece of grass. In the time it takes to relieve my bladder, the weather has taken a turn for the worse. The canoe wallows in the sheltered harbour, while, outside, wind and waves funnel down the narrow channel that separates the island from the mainland. It's a difficult call: do I sit tight and hope it's just a passing squall, or do I make a dash for it before it gets any worse? I take a chance and paddle like a lunatic straight for the mainland. Everything goes well until I reach midway, where the waves are high and breaking, and I experience a moment of pure terror. The canoe rises, crests and crashes over the surging waves. I pull and pound the paddle blades, just managing to break free of the frenzied waves still nipping at my heels. The relief is instantaneous, but the experience has left me rattled. I desperately want to get ashore and feel dry land beneath my feet. Forget completing the rest of the lough; it's time to call it a day.

'Concealed in this subtle wetlands habitat is a treasure trove of wildlife, rare breeding birds and unusual plants.'

When I do return to the water for the next leg of my journey, I decide to launch farther on downstream, bypassing where the river narrows and sweeps through Athlone. There is no particular need to put myself through the ordeal of portaging the canoe around the town's busy lock, and, besides, I'm much more interested in exploring the stretch of river that's about to unfurl.

The Shannon seems as keen as I am to head on south, as it pulls the canoe along at a surprising pace. Woodland, hedgerows and farmyards recede, and the landscape gently opens out into a flat and boundless plain, spreading away from the river as far as the eye can see. There are few trees and no signs of human habitation, no buildings or roads. The area is known as the Shannon Callows, and it represents the largest area of semi-natural grassland in the country. Callows derives from the Gaelic word *caladh*, meaning 'river meadow'. The Shannon Callows describes a region of floodplains that stretches from just below Lough Ree downstream to Lough Derg.

The river is heavy and meandering, swerving and looping in wide S-shaped bends. The landscape is fluid, a place where water and land blend seamlessly. Marshes, water meadows, ditches, water entering, water receding – and running through the heart of it the broad Shannon. Lush meadows slope gently to the river's edge, slowly submerging. Reed beds grow tall, dense and profuse along the margins. Concealed in this subtle wetlands habitat is a treasure trove of wildlife, rare breeding birds and unusual plants. Overhead, flocks of lapwings wheel and free-fall. Swans, duck and grebes paddle and graze in quiet backwaters. Pastures are flecked with huge varieties of flora, including cuckoo flowers, marsh bedstraw, common sedge, marsh pea and bog thistle. Also to be found are marsh marigold, meadowsweet, scabious, yellow loosestrife and orchids. In shallow ditches and pools, there is water mint, cress and forget-me-nots, along with yellow and white waterlilies.

Typically, flooding occurs in winter, with the low-lying pastures drying out in summer, when they are used for grazing and hay-making. The waterlogged plain has inhibited intensive farming – heavy machinery has trouble

accessing the fields, and the use of chemicals is discouraged. Because of its unique environment and traditional farming practices, the area experiences a greater diversity of plant life than anywhere else in the country. Grazing cattle keep in check the spread of willow and alders. Hay-cutting plays a crucial role in plant rejuvenation and grass management.

But like so many other parts of the world, the Callows are suffering the effects of climate change. Once upon a time this area was an important habitat in the conservation of the corncrake, which nested in meadows during the summer months. Increasingly, however, prolonged and late annual flooding has taken its toll on the bird, as heavy rains and rising waters have encroached on their breeding season, washing away their nests and denying them the chance to raise their brood. I'm about ten years too late to meet the corncrake. Late-summer flooding in 2010 wiped out the last of the area's breeding pairs – it now has the unfortunate title of being the first bird in Ireland to be made locally extinct because of climate change.

In spite of this great loss, the Callows are still an important avian refuge. In spring the meadows provide a feeding ground for migrating birds; summer is for breeding, and in winter, overwintering species arrive. It is a haven for skylarks, curlew, lapwing, redshank and snipe. It is possible to hear the calls of quail, wigeon, golden plover, black-tailed godwits, meadow pipits. Greenland white-fronted geese and whooper swans can be spotted in the winter months. Eighty per cent of the country's population of whinchats can be found in the Callows.

Plants and wildfowl are not the only ones who suffer from the floods. Farmers are inconvenienced and left wanting. Towns and homesteads can be marooned for weeks at a time.

'At a small indent, flocks of redshank and lapwings chatter and scamper like children on a beach.'

Time marches on, men lock horns, the crisis deepens. The ever-present river flows on, a charged and unpredictable force.

On this hot summer's day, the Shannon is burnished and potent. The stone-capped tower of Clonmacnoise teases in the distance. The river, weaving to and fro, keeps it just out of reach, until the full glory of the ancient monastic site is revealed at a break in the quivering reeds. The buildings occupy a slight rise, and are bounded by open meadowland and a few dishevelled hawthorn trees. It's impossible to resist their allure, and I paddle seamlessly from water onto land, beaching the canoe on a cushion of wild flowers – marsh pea, vetch and bird's-foot trefoil. Hired cruising boats jostle for space at the brimful jetty. A noisy convoy pulls in, crewed by a stag party of young, shirtless men, loud and beer-swilling. Confident that everyone needs to hear the lyrics of Limp Bizkit, they crank up the loudspeakers to maximum volume.

The monastic site is thronged with visitors, while a steady stream of tour buses deposits more groups at the entrance. The sight of so many people crowding together is off-putting, and the thought of turnstiles, interpretative centres and a gift shop selling trinkets is unappealing. I have had a good share of early Christian ruins already on my voyage – White Island and Devenish on Lough Erne, Inchcleraun and others yet to come. I'm content just to view Clonmacnoise from the shoreline, nibble some chocolate and try to ignore the rock festival.

On the river surges, as it widens, sprawling over the Callows, lapping at the hides of sleeping cattle. At a small indent, flocks of redshank and lapwings chatter and scamper like children on a beach. Fat and fluffy white clouds fill a cerulean sky. Reed beds quiver in the heat haze.

An ancient pilgrims' path leads away from the river as it cuts through the Callows and brings me to the entrance of Clonfert Cathedral. For just this once I may call myself a pilgrim while I seek out the shrine of Saint Brendan the Navigator, patron saint of boatmen, mariners, journey-makers, elderly adventurers, whales and canoe portage.

By far the most popular and enduring of the *immram* tales is St Brendan's epic voyage. The *Navigatio Sancti Brendani Abbatis* (Voyage of Saint Brendan the Abbot) recounts the tale, embellished and enhanced with wildly fantastical elements, of evangelical monks, led by Brendan, who build a currach and set out from the west coast of Ireland on an oceanic adventure in search of the Island of Paradise. The monks encounter a variety of bestiary – giant sheep, talking birds, a griffin, sea serpents and the gigantic whale Jasconius. They find shelter and adversity on a host of enchanted islands and come upon a cast of hermits and holy men. The text is heavily interwoven with references to the Catholic liturgical year, which the monks respect through fasting, purification and feasting. In the face of adversity and challenge, it is St Brendan whom the monks turn to for guidance and motivation, thus fostering the title 'Brendan the Navigator'.

The landscape of the *Navigatio* is fertile ground for conjecture. Reading between the lines, it is possible to interpret such features as icebergs, volcanoes and remote island landscapes. The Saint Brendan Society celebrates the belief that Brendan was the first European to reach North America, a thousand years before Christopher

Columbus. In 1976, the British explorer Tim Severin set out to test this theory. Severin built a boat that closely replicated St Brendan's own vessel. Sailing from Ireland with a crew of four, the expedition travelled up the Irish coast and took the traditional 'stepping stone' route across the North Atlantic, stopping off at the Faroe Islands and Iceland along the way. They arrived months later on Newfoundland's shores, proving that the *Navigatio* was indeed possible.

The veracity of Brendan's tale is unsupported, but it serves as a clever literary device. As word of his successful voyage spread, it drew thousands of pilgrims and students to seek the priest's wisdom and enlightenment, making Brendan an early Christian celebrity. Rich in metaphor and allegory, his tale appealed to a broad audience, and, as is customary of oral traditions, the story grew and changed. That he was an experienced overseas journey-maker is documented through his travels to Scotland, Wales, England and Brittany, where he endeavoured to spread the Christian message of faith, salvation and obedience.

Hard facts are in short supply when it comes to St Brendan's life story. He was born *c*. 484 near Fenit on the Kerry coast. His parents were members of the regional Altraige tribe, descendants of the noble Milesian race. His Gaelic name, *Braenfhionn*, means 'fine white mist', which is said to have descended during the child's naming ceremony. As was the custom for all children at the time, Brendan was removed from his parents during his first year and placed under the care of Sister Ita, who is said to have left a deep impression on the child whose early tutelage she managed. Once his formal studies were complete, Brendan returned to Kerry, where he was ordained a priest. Several minor miracles are attributed to him, but it is his tireless missionary work on behalf of the Roman Catholic Church that is formally documented. Early evangelical wanderings in his career saw him travelling by boat up the west coast of Ireland and across to Scotland, visiting remote island settlements along the way. His greatest legacy is Clonfert monastery, over which he presided as abbot. In its heyday the monastery accommodated up to 3,000 monks. St Brendan died at the hearty age of ninety-three, his body laid to rest in the grounds of his abbey.

A sign points the way to 'St Brendan's Tree'. The hinges of the iron gate squeak in protest when I push against it and step through into the cool darkness of an overgrown wood. A worn and crooked path leads to beneath a towering horse chestnut tree festooned with votive offerings – pieces of cloth, pairs of socks, rosary beads, asthma inhalers, matchboxes, coins, key fobs, children's toys and porcelain effigies of the Virgin Mary, all left by people seeking cures for sick children.

It takes several circuits of the medieval church's cemetery to find St Brendan's gravestone. On the verge of giving up, I finally notice a small plaque buried in the grass. The awkwardly phrased piece of polished limestone announces:

SAINT BRENDAN

484–578 A.D.

Abbot, Navigator and Confessor

BORN 484 A.D. TRALEE, CO. KERRY. ORDAINED A MONK 510 A.D. DIED 577–578 A.D. FOUNDED SCHOLASTIC MONASTERY AT CLONFERT 558 A.D. FIRST FOUNDATIONS AT ARDFERT, INIS-DADROIM, INCHIQUIN AND ANNAGHDOWN. GRAVE IS IDENTIFIED BY 'CATS PAWS' INDENTA-TIONS ON 'THE FLAT STONE SLAB'. HE SAILED FROM IRELAND WITH FOURTEEN MONKS IN AN EPIC VOYAGE TO DISCOVER THE NEW WORLD, LATER IDENTIFIED AS AMERICA.

An apple and some plastic-wrapped sweets have recently been left as offerings. Sure enough, the flat stone slab is there, complete with mysterious 'cats paws' markings. I had expected a more grandiose statement – a large shrine or worthy piece of sculpture – and hover around feeling slightly underwhelmed.

Saint Brendan's resting place sits in the shadow of the cathedral's entrance door, the once noble portal now a confusing jumble of Romanesque and recent stone carvings. The door is ajar, and the dark interior looks cool and inviting.

The Mermaid of Clonfert is an object of wonder and curiosity. The tiny stone carving is mischievously at odds in this hallowed setting, and I can't help smiling and giggling. From a distance she appears to be waving; she is in fact holding a comb aloft in one hand and a mirror in the other. Her exposed breasts have been buffed to a deep lustre by the touch of many wandering hands. She smiles back beguilingly.

What a strange place, I think to myself as I head back

down to the river. From the rag tree to the mermaid, nothing at Clonfert was quite as expected. I coax the canoe through the meadow and slip back into the river. I was born not far from here, a little farther downstream in a village called Terryglass at the top of Lough Derg. There's a tug of temptation to continue and seek out the place I left at the age of four and to which I haven't been back since. But I might just keep that adventure for another day. Shannon Harbour is a few minutes farther on downriver, and it's there my day's journey ends.

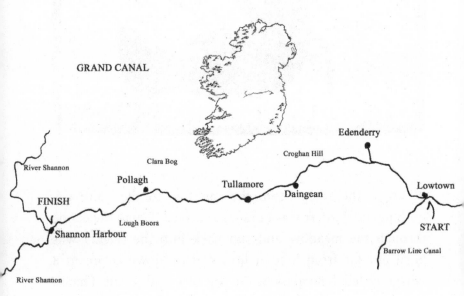

GRAND CANAL

River Shannon

Clara Bog

Croghan Hill

Edenderry

Pollagh

Tullamore

Daingean

Lowtown

FINISH

Lough Boora

START

Shannon Harbour

Barrow Line Canal

River Shannon

Waterlogged

I'm standing on the deck of a pedestrian bridge that spans the summit of the Grand Canal, overlooking a harbour ironically named Lowtown. The bridge has seen better days; its pre-stressed concrete is heavily pockmarked, and the corroded metal handrail looks as if it might crumble at the slightest touch. A raggle-taggle of boats is moored along the banks. The marina is host to a handful of traditional steel barges and narrowboats, but the majority are fibreglass, multi-storey cruisers. Several neglected vessels have given up hope of ever moving again, having sunk to the bottom. There's a thriving community of live-aboards here; potted plants, bicycles and wheelie bins clutter some of the upper decks, while washing lines of laundry flap in the breeze. An extreme version of a houseboat features a quirky garden shed lashed to a pallet raft, a wisp of smoke curling from the chimney of its wood-burning stove. Guerrilla gardening is happening along the towpath: giant sunflowers, runner beans and lettuce. A hand-painted sign bolted to the bridge's railing indicates ← R. *Shannon* and

Dublin → in big bold lettering. I slide *Minnow* down the bank and into the water and set off westwards downstream for Shannon Harbour.

The Grand Canal is a 131-kilometre man-made waterway. It climbs from sea level out of Dublin's city centre docklands and, like its Venetian namesake, navigates a dense cityscape of office blocks, apartments and hotels, ducking beneath the bridges of Portobello and Rialto. Freed from the urban sprawl, it ventures out across the once Great Bog of Allen, travelling languidly across the relatively level landscape of counties Kildare and Offaly, descending to meet the River Shannon near Banagher. Work began on its construction in the mid-eighteenth century, and took forty-seven years to complete. Thousands of labourers, known as 'navvies' (an abbreviation of the term 'navigators'), dug the canal channel entirely by hand, using primitive tools – picks, shovels and heavy wooden wheelbarrows. Tonnes of quarried limestone were used to build the forty-three locks and fourteen aqueducts and the numerous over-bridges. It was considered, at the time, to be one of the most ambitious public transport projects ever undertaken in the country. For at least a hundred years a steady stream of traffic used the canal, ferrying passengers and an assortment of goods along its course. It endured the devastating effects of the Great Famine, when the starving and the wretched thronged its banks, begging, and in some cases hijacking passing boats. It reclaimed its importance during the emergency years of the Second World War, when turf was shipped out of the Midlands to fuel the hungry capital. Increasing competition from rail and road forced the canal into decline and, by 1960, commercial traffic had ceased. Around this time, parts of the Grand Canal in Dublin were threatened with closure, destined either to be filled in or repurposed as a surface-water drain. These plans were thwarted by passionate campaigners, including the Inland Waterways Association of Ireland, the Irish Georgian Society, and my own father.

The canoe sits low in the water. It is packed to the gunnels with camping gear and several days' worth of provisions. Fresh drinking water is part of the heavy cargo, as clean sources are unreliable along this stretch of waterway. The extra ballast makes for heavier paddling, but I prefer the stability it gives the canoe. The towpath is busy with weekend joggers, walkers and children who want to say hello. I enjoy their innocent curiosity and happily answer their list of questions: 'Where are you going?' 'To the River Shannon.' 'What sort of boat is that?' 'It's a canoe.' 'Are you on your own?' 'Yes.' 'Do you get scared?' 'Yes.' A fleet of kayakers streaks past, members of a local paddling club engrossed in a punishing workout, the face of each paddler contorted in pain. I can smile smugly now, but in a few days, my own muscles will be feeling the burn. The persistent whine of the Mondello race-car track stalks me for the best part of an hour, and I paddle on quickly to escape the annoying sound. I encounter a VW Golf that has nosedived into the canal. The doors are all underwater and are still closed; any passengers must have escaped through the shattered rear window.

At the first whiff of turf smoke, I know I have passed into another realm. The unmistakable smell is so sweetly aromatic that as it fades away, I crave for more. At last, I settle into a rhythmic paddle, travelling steadily through

'At the first whiff of turf smoke, I know I have passed into another realm. The unmistakable smell is so sweetly aromatic that as it fades away, I crave for more.'

a quiet landscape along the deserted canal. The black-and-white gates of Ticknevin lock are visible in the distance. After a tricky portage I set out on the canal's lower level and a long stretch of lock-free water, arriving at Edenderry just in time for lunch.

At Edenderry harbour the quay is thronged with well-wishers of the avian kind – Barbary and mallard ducks. Skirmishes break out over crumbs and crusts, the discarded remains of my late lunch. The day is muggy and close as I return along a short canal spur that links Edenderry town to the main Grand Canal line. Milfoil grows thick and rampant in the shallow waterway. A towpath that runs parallel to our course has been freshly paved with tarmac, and is host to a steady stream of cyclists, joggers and pedestrians. Progress is staccato and slow because I get increasingly tangled up in weed or lured into conversation by curious passersby. By the time I reach the canal junction, I am feeling hot and bothered and pull in beneath the shade of a humpbacked roving bridge, wrestling off layers of clothing and gulping from a water bottle. Passing beneath the ancient horse portal, I rejoin the Grand Canal and follow the shimmering corridor into an Elysian world.

The rumble of motorway traffic subsides, cyclists run out of hard surface and turn back, joggers and dog walkers dwindle. Liberated from such early distractions, my senses grow attuned to this watery domain. I am now in the company of kingfishers, blackbirds, coots, thrushes, wrens, moorhens and herons. The clear water teems with fish; perch and pike streak ahead as *Minnow* cleaves a passage. Damselflies gather on the bow, hitching a lift downstream to fresh hunting ground.

The Bog of Allen is a catch-all name for a series of raised bogs concentrated in a band across the Irish Midlands, and the Grand Canal cuts right through its heart. It is a landscape that is easily overlooked. There is not the high drama of mountain ranges or the majestic sweep of rolling plains. It is a low, scrubby place with boundaries that are difficult to define, and is frequently dismissed as wasteland – drab, poor and monotonous. The soft substratum yields to weight and refuses to cooperate when any form of construction is attempted on its surface; roads pucker, rail tracks twist, buildings subside and canal banks crumble. Bogs were places to be feared and distrusted. They are tricky places to navigate, and many attempts have proven fatal.

'Bog' is derived from the old Irish word *bogach*, meaning 'soft ground'. The Irish were sometimes referred to by such derogatory terms as 'bog-trotters', 'bog-men' or 'bog Arabs'. Bogs were regarded as having a 'corrupt air' and being 'a retreat and harbour for malefactors'. Mysterious apparitions and supernatural beings are said to inhabit their watery domain. Bogs were places that I generally bypassed, so my expectations were low when I set off on this leg of the journey. I was unprepared for how deeply I would fall under an enchanting spell.

Time and distance slide by as I become caught up in the rhythmic strokes of the paddle. Dark clouds swell on the horizon, looking potentially thunderous. I grow anxious to make camp before the heavens open. Finding a place to pull in and safely leave the water is a constant challenge. Inevitably, the canal banks are too high and the water too deep for me to scramble ashore. On and on I paddle, until at last I find a small niche where the canal bank has partially subsided, making a perfect slipway for the canoe.

The canal sits on a high embankment, elevating it above the peaty plains. The towpath where I pitch my tent is a floriferous purple haze of devil's-bit scabious interwoven with specimens of meadowsweet, Queen Anne's lace, red and white clover, heath bedstraw, climbing bindweed and ling heather. Tall bulrushes, flag irises and bushy mare's-tail create a buffer between land and water. The linear garden hums with the sound of bumble and wild bees.

Brown hawkers and four-spotted chasers swoop in to inspect the newly arrived intruder. Of the thirteen species of dragonflies resident in Ireland, the largest and most powerful is the brown hawker. I am continually startled by its size. I can't help but feel unnerved each time I am visited by these miniature covert drones. The Swedish name for dragonfly is *Skams besman*, which roughly translates as 'Devil's steelyard'. According to folklore, the devil uses the insect, whose narrow, elongated body mimics a steelyard measure, to weigh a person's soul. As the dragonfly circles, it takes a measure of the individual's soul, and if the person is found wanting, they can expect serious injury to befall them in the near future. Aerial acrobats, dragonflies are able to hover, fly forwards, backwards and upside down. The beating wings of the four-spotted chaser make a distinct humming sound, not unlike a small mechanical drone.

While today the towpath is a rich and wild habitat, this was not always the case. Two hundred years ago it would have been a very different scene, with the path churned to a deep muddy pulp by the galloping hooves of horses. Fly boats were introduced on the Grand Canal in the nineteenth century. These light-weight express passenger ferries were towed by teams of three or four horses at a canter. The lead horse was ridden by a postilion, clad in a bright uniform. A daily service operated from Dublin to Tullamore, and this ninety-three-kilometre journey took an impressive nine hours and five minutes. In a good year, 100,000 people might have made the journey. A cook, a barmaid and a waitress were included as crew, and passengers were limited to one pint of wine on the voyage. Not only did the thundering hooves churn the path, but these speeding vessels would throw up a high wave, washing right over the banks. Goods' vessels were more sedate, and were pulled by teams of mules or draught horses. Horse-drawn vessels continued to use the towpath until the early twentieth century.

Exploring the bountiful flora, I am conscious of a deep, persistent mechanical hum, a white noise that permeates the atmosphere. Lured by the incessant sound, I slide down the embankment to investigate the source. I scramble through a dense hedge, and the scene that reveals itself is striking. Before me is a dark and barren plain, a black desert

'Before me is a dark and barren plain, a black desert stretching as far as the eye can see.'

stretching as far as the eye can see. Two huge tractors, the root cause of the persistent noise, traverse the length of this dark, flat plain. Trundling methodically along, they scrape away sections of the soft, black peat, harvesting this drained bog of its valuable raw material. The loose-milled peat is transported over long, narrow conveyor belts and spewed onto linear mounds. Where the harvesting has taken place, the bog is bare, black and as smooth as a billiard table. There is something hypnotic about the scene, and I remain transfixed by the maleficent vision for some time.

This seemingly inhospitable landscape remained relatively untouched for centuries. Evidence that some communities lived around the perimeter has been revealed through archaeological research. These early settlers availed of the rich habitat to satisfy their daily needs: hunting game, gathering berries and collecting mosses and bog cotton, which they used for bedding. From the seventeenth century onwards, pressure came to bear to develop the bogs for agricultural use. Localised efforts were made to drain the waterlogged wilderness, reclaiming it for livestock grazing and a source of fuel. Dried peat, or turf, was regarded as a valuable fuel commodity.

Mechanical harvesting dominated from the 1940s, as the demand for peat intensified. Two million tonnes were required annually to fuel a number of electricity-generating power stations based in the Midlands. The versatile raw material had many uses – as livestock bedding, brown wrapping paper, high-grade charcoal, insulation, firelighters, even soap, and, more recently, to manufacture peat briquettes. Other sites were drained and reclaimed for rough grazing pasture, forestry plantations and crop production. The peat industry shaped the social and economic landscape of the Midlands. It provided employment for thousands in a time of economic stagnation and mass emigration.

As our knowledge and understanding of this unique ecosystem grew, urgent measures for its protection and conservation were called for. Since the 1980s, the Irish Peatland Conservation Council has campaigned for the preservation of the country's remaining raised bogs. Peatland is now understood to be invaluable in mitigating climate change by removing and storing carbon dioxide from the atmosphere – hectare for hectare, a bog can store ten times more carbon than a forest. A healthy, living bog also helps with flood control, and is rich in biodiversity. Throughout Europe, attention is now being focused on rehabilitating cutaway bogs and preserving the last raised boglands.

At precisely five o'clock, the machines shudder to a halt, their grinding wheels and cogs muted as the workers knock off for the evening. A fine dust swirls and drifts over the landscape, and a deep silence settles. Soon all these machines will be permanently stifled, and nature will reclaim this bare, exploited landscape. Even now, in the verges of this desiccated bog, a new habitat thrives; birch, willow, sedges and grasses, pink heather and fluffy white wisps of bog cotton are waiting for an opportunity to colonise. As a consumer of peat, I have been complicit in this landscape's demise. For years I tossed briquettes into my stove, made liberal use of peat moss throughout my garden, and consumed electricity without a thought as to its origin. Pleading ignorance is a poor defence in these proceedings. As I write this, Bord na Móna, the dominant peat landlord, has formally ended peat extraction. Nevertheless, smaller local enterprises still continue to harvest.

I climb the bank and return to camp. With my back resting against *Minnow*'s upturned hull, I demolish a plate of rice and beans, disappointed yet again that I didn't cook a bigger meal. The sun dips below the horizon, and in the dwindling light I wash in the canal, dive into the tent and zip the door shut.

Twilight on the bog is when the Water Sheerie appears. The ghoulish shape-shifting demon presents itself as a pale light hovering over the bog, luring people to a watery grave. This mythical bog spirit is known throughout the world by many different names: in Brazil it is the *Boitatá*, or 'fiery serpent'; in Bangladesh it is the *Aleya*, the 'marsh ghost light'; and in England it is called Fool's Fire, or Jack-o'-lantern. John Milton wrote about it in *Paradise Lost*; Satan takes the form of a will-o'-the-wisp when he leads Eve to the Tree of the Knowledge of Good and Evil:

Kindled through agitation to a Flame,
Which oft, they say, some evil Spirit attends ...
Hovering and blazing with delusive Light,
Misleads th' amazed Night-wanderer from his way
To Bogs and Mires, and oft through Pond or Pool;
There swallow'd up and lost, from succour far.

This eerie light repeatedly appears in literary history, employed as a metaphorical reference to describe a hope that leads one on but remains impossible to reach. It is not just a figment of the imagination but an actual shimmering bioluminescence, a natural phenomenon believed to be caused by spontaneously combusting gases released from deep within the bog.

Cocooned inside the canvas dome, I lie awake, alert to the sounds of the bog. The atmosphere thickens with suspense. My fertile imagination is set on fire. Sound travels free and unchecked across the open plain. I hear the distinctive trumpeting of a cow calling to its calf, which is puzzling, since I know there is no such beast within range. A pair of ravens settles down to roost nearby and I eavesdrop on their pillow talk. Their conversation is cryptic; one bird's honk is low and repetitious, while the other's contribution is a curious tapping sound. Silence for a while, and then I hear a thrilling sound that makes my heart soar. It is the distinctive bubbling call of the curlew, a wonderful sound that rises and ripples out across the bog.

The native breeding curlew is on the verge of extinction in Ireland. Once a prolific and common species, its numbers have been in dramatic decline across Europe since the 1980s, and in Ireland the decline has been calamitous. Conservationists estimate that only 120 breeding pairs remain. Its Greek name, *Numenius*, meaning 'of the new moon', refers to the thin crescent shape of the bird's long bill. The curlew is our largest wading bird. It has an elegant body, long, stilt-like legs and an exceptional bill. Its tawny, mottled plumage is ideal camouflage in wilderness landscapes. The curlews' favoured habitat is bogland; they nest and feed in this habitat, using their long bills to probe watery pools for invertebrates. The bird's steep decline is due to a combination of factors. Drainage, excavation and afforestation of peatland has diminished its natural habitat, and intensification of farming has disrupted its breeding pattern. Being a ground-nesting bird, it is extremely vulnerable to predation from mammals such as foxes, badgers, mink and even crows, which demolish the delicate green eggs and juvenile hatchlings.

In 2016, Mary Colwell, a British nature writer, walked across Ireland and England to learn what she could about the plight of this much-loved bird. My kayaking adventure mirrors much of her route through Ireland. It was April when Mary began her odyssey on the shores of the River Erne in County Fermanagh. She passed through Enniskillen, the birthplace of her mother, and crossed the border into Cavan and Leitrim, broadly following the Shannon–Erne Waterway. Along the way she met individuals and organisations attempting to protect the curlew. With members of BirdWatch Ireland, she set out in a boat to explore the last nesting sites of the curlew on the Shannon. The final leg of her Irish pilgrimage took her along the towpath of the Grand Canal, from Shannon Harbour to Dublin. Her poignant journey is documented in her book *Curlew Moon*, published in 2018. She reveals how deeply rooted the curlew is in Ireland's culture and heritage.

A bird embedded in myth, eulogised in poetry and prose, the curlew is a symbol of life and rejuvenation. In her book's closing chapter, Colwell voices the significance of this beloved bird, and why every effort must be made to ensure its conservation:

Birds like curlews have contributed so much to our cultural, scientific, aesthetic and spiritual lives, and inspire so much of what makes us human. To lose them would be to diminish ourselves, and to diminish our ability to express what we feel so deeply.

'The future of this "new moon" bird hangs in the balance, though, and there is still a very real possibility that the curlew will be extinct in Ireland within the next five to ten years.'

A Curlew Task Force was established in direct response to Colwell's efforts. Managed by the Department of National Parks and Wildlife Services, the group comprises farmers, conservationists, foresters, turf-cutters and academics all working to reverse the bird's decline. The future of this 'new moon' bird hangs in the balance, though, and there is still a very real possibility that the curlew will be extinct in Ireland within the next five to ten years. I knew the chances of sighting this rare bird on my journey would be slim, and I hardly dared to hope that I would hear one. My ear strains to hear the bubbling call as it recedes into the darkness. It is a bittersweet moment that I will recall for many months to come.

Sleep comes slowly as my mind actively replays all the day's sights, sounds and experiences. The towpath turns out to be the most comfortable piece of earth I have ever camped on, a soft and perfectly sprung natural mattress on which I doze contentedly. Occasionally I am startled by sounds of energetic splashing in the water beside me. A fish leaping out maybe, or a frog diving in? I rise at dawn, keen to continue travelling deeper into the bog. Snails and slugs have been busy exploring my camp overnight; their slime trails coat the tent's outer sheet, and *Minnow*'s hull too. I pack quickly and slide back into the water as the sun lifts into the sky.

The clarity of light and air is piercing. The sense

of isolation is thrilling. I feel like an explorer travelling through undiscovered lands. I find my rhythm quickly and paddle steadily westwards through the morning. Herons startle out of the reeds with deafening screeches and clumsy wing-flapping, their gangly legs akimbo. Over several kilometres I play chase and flee with a kingfisher, the canoe's perpetual motion pushing the bird farther and farther along the waterway – or maybe there's more than one bird, I never can tell.

I glide beneath the arches of old stone bridges. When driving in a car, it is easy to overlook these fine feats of engineering, but from the water the perspective is entirely different – their functional, elegant lines and correct proportions make them easy on the eye. Scalloped ridges are carved into the limestone arches through the friction of wet and dirt-laden tow ropes over many, many years. Built to carry the traffic of the time (pedestrians, carts and animals), today they bear the weight of heavy goods lorries, tractors and cars, an enduring testament to their craftsmanship.

Traffic lights are not something I ever thought I would encounter on a canal, so I am surprised when one comes into view. Beyond the signal is a lifting bridge that carries a light railway across the canal, part of a vast network of rail tracks that shunt trolley-loads of harvested peat across the bog. The bridge is raised open as I make the long approach, but an earsplitting alarm erupts suddenly, and the traffic light, which had been green, turns red. The bridge drops closed like a clam shell, and *Minnow* and I drift, curious to see what will pass. Nothing crosses, and the bridge shudders open again after the traffic light turns green. I paddle under and out the other side, puzzling over this surreal experience.

The canal skirts the western slopes of Croghan Hill, the remains of an extinct volcano. The hill stands almost at the centre of the Bog of Allen, and is a distinctive landmark in this low-lying plain. In pagan times it was the site of royal inaugurations and, naturally, it is also steeped in mystery and folklore. *Brí Éile* is the hill's Gaelic name and, according to one ancient tale, it was home to a young woman called Éile, a member of the fairy people who lived within the mound. Éile's beauty was so powerful that the men of Ireland fought one another to win her hand in marriage. Every year at *Samhain*, when the fairy mounds were open to common mortals, men would come to the hill in search of Éile and the prospect of wooing her. But fairy people are notoriously mischievous, and they exacted a heavy price for such romancing. For every man who tried to win Éile, one of his comrades would die mysteriously.

In May 2003, a digger was excavating in a bog at the foot of the hill when it scooped up in its bucket the partial remains of a human body. Old Croghan Man, as he became known, had lain preserved in the bog for over 2,000 years. He is one of many bog bodies recovered from peatlands across Europe, the vast majority of which date from 400 BC to AD 400. The acidic condition of the peat acts like a pickling agent, naturally mummifying the skin, organs

'The acidic condition of the peat acts like a pickling agent, naturally mummifying the skin, organs and hair of the individual's corpse.'

and hair of the individual's corpse. Following the discovery, Old Croghan Man underwent months of intense analysis. The body was determined to have been that of a man in his twenties. He was tall in stature and possibly of regal birth; his fingernails were neatly manicured and his hands show little evidence of manual labour. The contents of his stomach revealed a last meal of buttermilk and grain. Bogs were regarded as sacred places by the early pagan Irish, who held complex beliefs that featured multiple gods and goddesses. Votive offerings were cast into the watery domains to appease the gods of fertility and harvest. The fact that Old Croghan Man was recovered on an ancient tribal boundary suggests a possible link with rituals of kingship and sovereignty. Analysis of the corpse revealed that he was the victim of ritualistic torture, and quite possibly a human sacrifice. A deep stab wound to the chest killed him, and he was then decapitated and his torso cut in half. A number of incisions were discovered on the chest. Withies, a type of rope made from thin, twisted hazel rods, were threaded through his upper arms.

Several of Ireland's bog bodies, including Old Croghan Man, are displayed at the National Museum of Ireland in Dublin. I visited the exhibition some weeks after my journey along the Grand Canal. Under subdued lighting, Croghan's severed and decapitated remains lie enshrined in a glass tomb. Entering the small enclosed space that shrouds the body, I experienced a sharp involuntary intake of breath as my eyes settled on the man's remains. The body's skin has a stiff, leathery texture, and is deeply tanned, stained by the dark-brown peat in which he lay. His hands are almost perfectly preserved. The natural creases of the palms, wrists and curled fingers are clearly defined. Cuticles and fingernails have been meticulously conserved. My gaze flits over the mutilated torso, a shrivelled bag of skin, the skeletal bones having long ago disintegrated. A thinly plaited leather amulet loosely encircles the man's upper left forearm; I focus on this object and try to still my mind. It is a disturbing sight to behold, visceral and shocking. With a creeping sense of being a voyeuristic fool, I bolt from the scene.

Bog bodies are not unique to Ireland. The preserved remains of men, women and adolescents have been recovered from bogland sites in Germany, England, Denmark and the Netherlands. Each corpse is named after the particular location where they were discovered – Tollund Man (Denmark), Windeby Girl (Germany), Lindow Man (England), Yde Girl (Netherlands), to list just four. Almost all suffered a violent end, strangled, hanged, stabbed, sliced or beaten to death. 'Triple death' often features. Did they give their lives in punishment, were they victims of crime or was there a sacrificial purpose to their deaths? Could those who placed the bodies in the waterlogged ground have known they would be preserved for millennia to come?

Many of the exhibition artefacts on the National Museum's ground floor have been recovered from Irish bogs, and they are easier on the eye and make for far less uncomfortable viewing than the bodies. Among them is the colossal Lurgan canoe (c. 2500 BC) recovered from Addergoole Bog in County Galway. Fifteen metres long, it was honed from the trunk of a single oak tree. Tools, weapons, articles of clothing, decorative pieces of jewellery and even hunks of butter have been uncovered in bogs throughout the country.

According to my Waterways Ireland guide, the town of Daingean is an hour's paddle away. I'm looking forward to reaching it because I will be joined by a friend, Mandy, who is going to cycle along the towpath beside me for the next few days. I paddle into Daingean ahead of time and set out to explore this little urban oasis. In the course of its history, the town underwent several name changes. It started life as Fort Governor, a stronghold established by the English in the sixteenth century. As its status grew, it took the name of Philipstown, in honour of Mary Tudor's husband, King Philip II of Spain. Such was its prosperity and significance, it was represented at Parliament in London by two MPs. Following Ireland's independence, Philipstown was renamed Daingean, the origins of which derive from the Gaelic *Daingean Ua bhFáilghe*, meaning 'fortress of the Uí Fáilghe clan', the region's Celtic overlords.

Today just two boats are moored against the old quay wall beneath the crooked bridge. If my guidebook is to be believed, somewhere nearby there should be a tap supplying drinking water to users of the canal. I find the tap, but it is lifeless, sabotaged by vandals. Still wearing my life jacket and high-vis jacket, I wander the town's broad main street in search of a shop with bottled water. A popular supermarket chain store had a presence here, but now it too is out of action, its windows boarded up and a 'For Sale' notice swinging from the eaves. Many other buildings along the street are also closed and advertised for sale. Despite the ghostly atmosphere, Daingean retains a certain charm, and efforts are being made to attract visitors and improve the town's fortunes. Work is underway to upgrade the towpath to a cycleway – a continuation of the Grand Canal Greenway, linking Dublin to the west.

My friend arrives and we unload her bike, then she sets off on a potholed track while I return to smooth water. We struggle initially to find a pace that suits both paddler and cyclist. With no headwind and weed-free water, I can average a speed of roughly six kilometres an hour, too slow for a cyclist, too fast for a walker. Eventually we settle on a rate, and a steady stream of gossip keeps us entertained for the next few hours. A family of mute swans emerges from beneath Ballycommon Bridge, parents with seven cygnets in tow. It is always a tense moment when encountering these huge birds in such narrow confines. The cobs, in particular, tower over the canoe's low perspective. I try to give them as wide a berth as possible, but the adults still puff out their feathers and hiss their disgust. Below the bridge we stop briefly at the junction with another canal spur, long closed to boating traffic. Numerous canal branches were constructed off the main canal line; these waterways benefited lesser regional towns and helped rural communities prosper. This canal branch leads to Kilbeggan, a town thirteen kilometres to the north. It was closed to navigation in 1961, and a dam was placed at its junction to the main canal line. Over the decades its channel has been reclaimed by nature, but plans are underway to restore it. Local community groups in Kilbeggan and Ballycommon are already working to restore the towpath for walkers and potentially for cyclists.

Near the junction, a large steel boat is moored, a relic of the traditional cargo vessels that once plied the waterways.

It was on board this type of vessel that I first experienced the canal as a small child. During the 1960s and 1970s, my father, who has a keen interest in waterway heritage, part-owned two traditional canal boats – hulking twenty-tonne steel monsters with the decidedly unromantic names of *76M* and *42B*. Working boats on Irish canals were assigned numbers, and were rarely 'named'; *76M* was built in 1937 for the Grand Canal Company. Their cavernous holds transported goods – turf, bricks, stone, grain and much more besides – along the Grand Canal and River Barrow for decades. Later on, my parents downsized to a succession of narrowboats, brightly painted vessels of the type commonly seen on English canalways. I have few memories of these halcyon days; the only evidence is a handful of dog-eared photographs, which show me trussed in a bulky orange life jacket, too small even to reach the boat's tiller.

Mandy and I move on and approach our first lock, one of a series of steep descents that we'll encounter in the next few days. As we get ready to portage around the obstacle, the resident lock-keeper appears. James 'Jimmy' Fisher insists we both come into his house for a cup of tea. In his spotless kitchen he serves us 'lock-keeper tea'. I had heard stories about this legendary brew, and was keen to experience it. The tea is jet black and as thick as tar. I glance at Mandy, who is staring at her mug in horror; I may have failed to fill her in on this aspect of the journey. During the canal's heyday a lock-keeper was assigned to each lock. It was a twenty-four-hour job, because cargo boats travelled through the night, and each keeper was provided with a cottage beside the lock. Today there are ten lock-keepers, or 'Water Patrollers', as they are now officially called, to manage the forty-seven locks along the Grand Canal. I would like to spend longer in Jimmy's kitchen sharing stories, but with four more locks to confront, we must get a move on. Besides, I can feel my gums retreating painfully from the tannic brew.

With Mandy's help, we make light work carrying the canoe around the lock. The next four locks pass in quick succession, and we travel farther along the canal than anticipated. Exiting at our fifth lock, we find a wide area of manicured grass that looks perfect for our tents, but just as we are about to unpack, a dishevelled man and a dirty collie dog appear at our side. The hapless man bursts into a flurry of animated and incoherent chatter. He is evidently high on drugs and is definitely drunk. Mandy and I take one look at each other and wordlessly decide to continue on, leaving man and dog hopping and barking on the towpath. Away in the distance the bright lights of Tullamore beckon through a fine drizzle. While it has been a productive day on the water, after twenty-five kilometres and seven lock portages, I am exhausted and paddling erratically. We pull in and shake out our tents on a lonely stretch of hard canal bank.

I sleep badly and spend the morning stumbling over tent pegs groggily and dribbling toothpaste down my front. Mandy, on the other hand, bounds out of her tent bright-eyed and energetic, like a golden retriever. We break camp and continue our journey along the canal, dropping down through yet more locks. Approaching the outskirts of Tullamore, the canal widens and is flanked by a long line of poplar trees. Under the clear blue sky we are transported momentarily to the Canal du Midi in southern France. The tree-lined bank yields abruptly to a busy urban centre.

Tullamore owes its existence to the Grand Canal, which flows through it. A reference to the town in the 1780s described it as 'a very mean village with scarce any better houses than thatched cabins'. By 1830, after the canal's arrival, it had become an important market town, boasting a distillery, a brewery, brick factories and several hotels. As canal trade and traffic declined from the 1940s onwards, the town turned its back on the canal. When the English canal explorer Hugh Malet passed through Tullamore in the late 1950s on board his leaky boat, the *Mary Ann*, he described crumbling warehouses, a weed-filled harbour basin and a general state of decay. I linger at the place where Malet moored *Mary Ann*; the original buildings, the towering warehouses and hotels have been demolished, but the space today is clean and well maintained. Several narrowboats and fibre-glass cruisers are moored against the cut-stone quay. In 2013, the sunken remains of five cargo boats were resurrected from the harbour floor. The peaty canal waters had preserved their steel hulls, in a similar manner to that of the bog bodies. The vessels were sold for restoration, and some were converted into houseboats.

Tullamore is anything but 'mean' or sad this morning. Life at street level looks frantic and fast: gangs of children are heading back to school after their long summer break, there's a cacophony of jackhammers, car horns and security alarms. The noise and hectic human activity are a shock to the senses. Mandy's cycle lane diverges from the canal and we lose sight of each other for a while. I paddle on in a bewildered state, slipping beneath and between steel and concrete structures. In the town's centre, the canal drops through two locks and, because they are so closely staged, we combine them in one long portage. In doing so, we have to carry *Minnow* across a busy main road, much to the surprise and irritation of the early-morning commuters. Mandy spies a service station, and while she stocks up on sausage rolls and murky grey tea, I explore the novel delights of a flushing toilet and hot running water. Returning to the canalside, we gorge on our spoils like two ravenous feral dogs.

Back on the water and paddling westwards, the noise and commotion recede and we embrace the solitude of our watery domain. The canal takes us past the crumbling ruins of Srah Castle, a legacy of Ireland's Jacobite past. On cue, a pair of ravens emerge and circle the building's fragmented ramparts. Rounding a bend, I am hit with a strong headwind, and the extra effort to maintain progress makes its presence felt in the muscles of my arms and shoulders. Another lock looms, and I think about lunch and a long paddle break. Just as I step ashore, two Waterways Ireland boatmen introduce themselves and persuade me to descend through the lock. I have travelled through locks many times on narrowboats and barges, but never in a tiny open canoe. Having heard horror stories of canoes capsizing and sinking in lock chambers, I am reluctant to try it out, but the men assure me it will be an easy process, while Mandy goads me on.

I grudgingly return to the water, paddle into the lock chamber and cling resolutely to a thick chain tethered to the wall. The gates close behind me and the men raise the sluices to empty the watery chamber. The level drops steadily and *Minnow* and I sink with it, my hands slipping down the slimy length of chain, which I'm terrified to release, convinced the canoe will be sucked into the gurgling vortex. We reach the bottom of the deep trough, where the air is chilly and damp, and water seeps from secret crevices. Behind me the heavy gates creak beneath the weight of dammed water, and I feel extremely vulnerable.

Invertebrates and other tiny aquatic creatures scuttle across the now exposed walls. As I reach the level of the lower canal, the men heave open the gates and I paddle swiftly out into bright sunshine. The entire process took minutes, with no effort on my part; how much easier the journey would be if I could repeat this process at every lock.

'Behind me the heavy gates creak beneath the weight of dammed water, and I feel extremely vulnerable.'

We stop for lunch at Huband Aqueduct, overlooking the skeletal remains of Ballycowan Castle. It feels good to stretch stiff legs. My goal for the day is to reach Henesy's Bridge, roughly six kilometres farther along the canal, and make camp there before night falls. Returning to the water, I battle into a strong headwind. The channel acts like a wind tunnel. In certain gusts I paddle on the spot, struggling just to hold my own against the wind. The banks are thick with bulrushes. I now understand why it is referred to as 'spindle of the banshee' – the shrieking wind-lashed foliage makes conversation impossible, and Mandy and

I fall silent, heads bent against the relentless force of the wind. Moorhens, startled into half-flight, skitter across the rippled water, their spindly yellow feet splashing frantically over the surface. Kingfishers zigzag from bank to bank. My arms and shoulder muscles burn, but I must paddle on. The Thatch pub, an infamous watering hole for canal boatmen, comes into view. Thoughts of a toasted ham and cheese sandwich, washed down with a pot of tea, invade my head. We pull in and find that the pub is shuttered up and lifeless, another sorry victim of rural decline. Moored against the old jetty are two weed-harvesting boats. I sidle alongside for a closer look and am greeted by the boats' operators, who are keen to strike up a conversation. They are canal maintenance workers, employees of Waterways Ireland. Weed-cutting along the Grand Canal is continuous from May until September. They explain how the boats operate in pairs: the lead boat cuts the weeds along the canal channel, while the follow-on boat collects the cut material and pushes it up against the banks, where it decays. This process keeps the canal waters flowing, allowing boats to travel without getting their propellers fouled. It also benefits the wildlife, encouraging and increasing the channel's biodiversity, which, if left unmanaged, would quickly become a weed-choked ditch.

As we say our goodbyes, one of the men darts inside his wheelhouse, grabs a cushion off the driver's seat and presents it to me with a flourish (I may have complained about a numb backside). The cushion is hideous, green velvet, edged with ratty gold brocade, but I am touched by this spontaneous act of generosity. Sitting regally on my overstuffed padding, I wobble off into the wind.

My arms and shoulders are truly on fire by the time we arrive at the last lock of the day. I'm pretty sure I've torn a tendon while lifting the canoe in and out of the canal. We pitch our tents on a narrow patch of grass beside the deep lock chamber. I brew a saucepan of tea and drink it quickly to quench a raging thirst. The lock-keeper's cottage, on the opposite bank, is a pretty building. Its walls are thickly whitewashed, its wooden sash windows painted a cheerful scarlet. My father remembers the place as 'Watty's lock'. I mention this to the current lock-keeper, Alan, who comes out to meet us. Watty (Walter), it turns out, was Alan's grandfather. I am amazed to discover that Alan is an eighth-generation lock-keeper, and his young son is set to be the ninth. His six times great-grandfather, James Mitchell, was involved in the construction of the canal in the eighteenth century, and was promoted to the role of lock-keeper when boats first used the waterway. Alan is keen to talk about the canal, and he tells me that there has been a marked decline in the amount of traffic passing through the locks in recent years. He remembers helping over a thousand boats lock through in 2007, while this year fewer than 300 boats have passed. As he departs, he warns us that a storm is due late tonight and tomorrow. I look at our tents pitched right at the edge of the deep lock chamber and have a nightmarish vision of being swept into the canal in the dead of night. Too late now. Mandy and I double-check the tent pegs and cross fingers that they will hold.

I crawl into my sleeping bag and swallow a cocktail of painkillers, washed down with a nip of whiskey in the hopes that it will relieve the aches and pains. A chill wind whips and worries the tent canvas while I lie awake and think about the ebb and flow of this canal's fortunes. In England the canals teem with boats, sometimes to the point of gridlock at the height of summer. On this leg of my journey, I have met just three boats and four canoes. I drift in and out of consciousness, unable to blot out the bombastic roar of the locks' overflow, which could easily compete with the Niagara Falls.

Despite the thunderous rain clouds that are brewing, I feel compelled to take to the water the following morning; some strange force lures me on. Mandy has retrieved her car and we rip down the tents and fling our gear into the boot. The guidebook tells me there are two locks ahead and then a long straight run to a place called Pollagh. With *Minnow* empty of cargo, she should fly through the water and make it to Pollagh before the heavens open.

Between the two of us we jog the canoe past the locks. A burly black Labrador ambushes us with deep-throated growls and barks. We shout down the angry beast, which turns tail in fright, melting into the dark ditch. Back on the water, I round the final bend and stare down the barrel of the poker-straight canal. Somewhere at its end lies Pollagh. At first the rain is just a fine drizzle, light pitter-patters on the water surface, and then all hell breaks loose. The rain is torrential; stair-rods pierce the surface all around me. I paddle like a woman possessed, my arms moving like a flywheel, pushing *Minnow* like never before. The canalscape disappears behind sheets of rain, leaving me with no clue as to my progress. Cold water fills the canoe, and soon I am sitting in a deep, sloshing pool. Fear makes me stop and bail, but this is a pointless exercise, so I paddle on and let the water rise. I can hardly keep my eyes open in the stinging rain, and the paddle is slick and slippery in my hands. The violent strokes of the blade disturb a sleeping pike, causing it to leap out of the water and slam its body against *Minnow*'s hull. A split-second glimpse of the fish's huge, serrated teeth pitches me into hysterical laughter.

At last, Pollagh swims into focus and I glide beneath the shelter of the village's only bridge, shivering and gulping for air. I urgently need to get out of these cold and saturated clothes. I scramble up the slippery bank, hauling *Minnow* behind me, and turn her keel-side up on the grassy towpath. Back beneath the bridge, among the broken glass bottles, cigarette butts and empty crisp packets, I strip off drenched layers and struggle into dry spares, with which Mandy has arrived.

In the driving rain the tiny village is deserted. A handful of buildings are spread out over a wide area on either side of the canal – a church, a small national school and a pub that looks as if it hasn't served customers in quite a while. Pollagh is derived from the Gaelic name *Pollach*, meaning 'place full of holes', a reference to the village's boggy origins. Before the canal arrived, the area was wild and uninhabitable, with 'pools so deep you could drown a horse' in them. In the eighteenth century a seam of blue-grey clay, known locally as 'lackleagh', was discovered beneath the peat around these parts. The clay's properties made it suitable for brickmaking, and a thriving cottage industry soon took root. At least thirteen brickyards operated in the village – small, family-run businesses. The work was laborious, backbreaking and pitiful. Every member of the household was involved: men, women and children as young as eight years old. 'Dog bricks' were unique to the area. Local hounds would run across the drying bricks, their paw prints leaving an indelible impression in the damp clay. Turf was cut from the surrounding bog to fire the kilns. The baked clay resulted in distinctive yellow bricks, which were loaded onto barges and shipped to Dublin. At its peak, in the 1840s, up to four million bricks a year were transported out of Pollagh along the canal.

I learn all this at the community centre, where we take shelter from the rain, bracing ourselves on a tilting leatherette sofa, nursing mugs of milky tea. A communal bookshelf offers works in two genres, crime and romance. I lose myself in a bodice ripper while Mandy scrolls her phone. Uncertain if or when the rain will clear, Mandy decides to head for home. I have really enjoyed her company, and feel reluctant to continue on alone. I stow my gear under *Minnow*'s hull and retreat to the sanctuary of a lemon-yellow church to contemplate my options.

The heavy door yields and I step inside a hallowed hall exploding in fantastic light. The sources of the kaleidoscopic colour are two slim stained-glass windows behind the altar: Christ the Redeemer cloaked in crimson and the Blessed Virgin Mary draped in mauve and blue, a dagger piercing her heart. The intensity of colour, the rich and intricate detail of the work is awe-inspiring. Dark, damp thoughts instantly evaporate as I stand in admiration of this stunning work. The windows are attributed to the renowned Harry Clarke Studios, though not the handiwork of the man himself. They were commissioned a few years after the artist's untimely death. The windows are not the only objects of wonder in the building. The altar and tabernacle are uncommon and intriguing. Formed out of bog yew by the artist Michael Casey, these gnarly pieces of wood were pulled from the bog, where they lay preserved for over four thousand years. Honed and polished, the wood reveals its story, the sinuous forms a primordial tale of wonder.

'Honed and polished, the wood reveals its story, the sinuous forms a primordial tale of wonder.'

Weatherbound and restless, I sift through brochures back at the community centre. A tri-fold flyer advertising the Clara Bog Nature Reserve catches my attention. The introduction boldly claims it to be 'one of the best remaining examples of a relatively intact raised bog in

Western Europe'. Having witnessed the drained and barren tracts of harvested bog earlier in the voyage, I resolve to make the effort to experience a living one.

The deluge has passed and the atmosphere is clear and bright when I step out on the raised-timber boardwalk that wends its way over the small oasis of Clara Bog. The eye sweeps loose and free over the boundless terrain. What strikes me first are the colours, a late-summer mantel of warming ochre, shot through with russet, malt, chartreuse, scarlet and hoary grey. Its ethereal pools are the colour of cask-aged whiskey. A living mat of sphagnum moss sits over the watery domain. It looks soft and inviting, and I wrestle a childish urge to jump onto the wobbly surface. The brochure, which I keep clutched in my hand, is peppered with fascinating facts and details about the bog. During the Second World War, sphagnum was harvested from it, its antiseptic properties useful in the treatment of wounds. Samples of Clara moss have travelled to the International Space Station, apparently; its extraordinary ability to survive in extreme conditions, without light or air, is of interest to scientists as a potential growth medium for producing food in outer space. Sphagnum comes in many varieties, and each one creates a unique micro-habitat, giving rise to the characteristic features of a raised bog: hummocks, lawns, flushes, soaks and pools.

To get a closer look at a bog's micro-habitat, you must sink to its level. Sprawling, belly-down on the boardwalk, with my face hovering just above the surface, I encounter a fantastic miniature world of plants and animals. At first it appears as a confusing mass but, in time, the eye begins to unpick details from the tangled web. Tiny wands of cranberry are entwined with low woody specimens of bog rosemary, which in turn blends into brittle shoots of cowberry. Leafy fronds of bog myrtle protrude randomly. Antler lichen forms delicate, lace-like patterns on dry hummocks. Tufts of purple moor grass are studded with scabious. Lurking in here somewhere are flesh-eating plants: sundews, bladderworts and butterworts. I locate a specimen of oblong sundew, its lime-green tongues extending upwards through a patch of blood-red sphagnum. Though its flowering season has long since passed, battered wisps of bog cotton endure.

'Lurking in here somewhere are flesh-eating plants: sundews, bladderworts and butterworts.'

Dizzy from the blood that pools in my head as I hang over the boardwalk's edge, I roll onto my back and focus on the sky. Ideally what I need to explore this habitat effectively is a magnifying glass or macro lens. Similar thoughts must have run through the mind of Mary Ward, the pioneering microscopist who grew up not far from here. Mary was born into a life of privilege and wealth in 1827, close to Ferbane. Armed with a magnifying glass, she explored the open landscape and grounds around her home, absorbed by a world of tiny plants and creatures. Relatives and friends recognised and encouraged the young girl's interests. When she turned eighteen, she received a present of a microscope. Entirely self-taught, she quickly mastered the state-of-the-art instrument, preparing her own slides from thin slivers of ivory. Returning from expeditions, Mary would place collected specimens under the microscope and transfer her observations into watercolour studies. Her studies and illustrations ranged from otter hair follicles and eel scales to cross-sections of a fish's eyeball. Keen to share her research, she set about publishing her work in book form. Because it was so difficult to find a publisher willing to accept manuscripts from women, her first book, *Sketches with the Microscope in a Letter to a Friend*, was privately printed. All two hundred and fifty copies sold out within the year and, such was the demand, it was reissued the following year by a London publishing house, re-entitled *A World of Wonders Revealed by the Microscope*. The book went on to be reprinted eight times between 1858 and 1864. Mary Ward's curious mind explored the world of astronomy too. As a frequent visitor to Birr Castle (her cousin was the 3rd earl of Rosse), she had the opportunity to document the building of the world's largest telescope, 'The Leviathan'. In 1859, her second book, *Telescope Teaching*, was published. Written and illustrated by the author, it is a guide to the night sky, describing constellations, moons, planets and the path of comets. Mary Ward's achievements are all the more significant since this was a time when women were rarely educated beyond the subject of domestic science – libraries and laboratories were off limits for them, they were unable to obtain degrees or certification from universities and they were denied membership of any learned societies.

I return to my own field studies and watch an enormous furry brown caterpillar curl itself around a woody stem; later I identify it as the larva of a fox moth. Having spotted one, I start to see them everywhere – the place is crawling with them! There's a seductive force in action here. Absorbed and distracted in an earthly paradise, the bog lures me in and down. I delve a hand into a trough and stir the contents, hoping to excite lurking creatures. A putrid stench rises, gaseous and sharp. I pull back quickly, as though I've been stung.

'So fragile is this ecosystem that the slightest intervention can upset the balance.'

In the 1980s attempts were made to drain this bog and make way for peat harvesting. Its fate was almost sealed when a last-minute intervention by a concerned public secured its reprieve. So fragile is this ecosystem that the slightest intervention can upset the balance. Work is continuing to prevent the bog from drying out and subsiding. Today, Clara Bog and its associated visitor centre provide a vital insight into this precious habitat.

I complete the looped walk and snatch hasty images on my camera, recording as many elements as possible for later study. In the camera's final frame, the lens focuses on something ghastly floating in a dark pool, a used baby's nappy. Heading back to Pollagh and my waiting canoe, I obsess about the nappy. The careless disregard makes my blood boil, and then I recall reading somewhere that sphagnum moss was used in ancient times as a natural nappy, and marvel at the irony.

I paddle away from Pollagh, which has, for a time, become the centre of my universe. A long stretch of lock-free waterway takes me through Boora and Turraun bogs, the last of the great peat plains. Until the beginning of the twentieth century, raised bog blanketed the countryside for several thousand hectares. Small-scale peat production grew to industrial proportions, and by the 1980s most of the landscape had been drained and cut away. A stripped raised bog cannot be restored to its former glory, but it can be rehabilitated and given a new lease of life. Drains can be blocked, allowing the peat to become waterlogged again, and nature can be encouraged to colonise. An ambitious example of this approach is the Lough Boora Parklands, 3,000 hectares of open area bordering the Grand Canal. I have a particular desire to visit Lough Boora, not only to witness how nature has successfully reclaimed it, but also to visit its renowned sculpture park.

Ever since the German avant-garde artist Joseph Beuys, visiting Ireland in the 1970s, exhibited *Irish Energy* (two peat briquettes sandwiched together with butter), Irish bogs have been the subject of some exciting and provocative contemporary artworks. In 2002, seven artists were invited to participate in a three-week residency at Boora Bog. Their brief: to create site-specific works of art inspired by the landscape and the region's industrial heritage. Several of the pieces resulting from the residency now form part of the Lough Boora Parklands permanent collection. The collection has expanded over the years, with leading artists such as Eileen MacDonagh, Alan Counihan, Patrick Dougherty and Naomi Seki creating monumental works influenced by the unique landscape.

If I could choose only one exhibition highlight, it would have to be *Boora Convergence*, a piece by David Kinane. The work is modelled on the familiar water-cooling towers of Ferbane power station, whose hungry furnaces were fed by Boora peat. The soaring sculpture is built of steel and wood, salvaged from railway tracks that carried away the harvested peat. It is an elegant and airy form that rises like a vortex out of the ground, vanishing high into the sky. I sink onto the spongy peat floor and reflect on the sculpture's multi-layered references.

The long-term legacy of this canal's construction is the demise of the great Bog of Allen. Despite warnings to the contrary, the engineers were determined to build the canal through the bog. Their principal reasoning was that it would be easier and quicker to excavate a channel through the soft peat than over or around it. From the moment the navvies slung their picks, the area came under threat. The building of the channel acted as a barrier, inhibiting the natural circulation of water within the bog. In places, where the canal crosses, the bog has sunk as much as thirteen metres, a process that continues to this very day. That said, the canal has established itself as an

important habitat for nature – it is teeming with life above and below the waterline. In recent years there is growing recognition of its value and importance as a public amenity and recreational resource.

Hives! Hundreds of raised red and angry bites cover my legs, backside and stomach – I must have been attacked by something when I sat down in Boora Bog. My arrival into Shannon Harbour is undignified and inglorious, as I squirm and wiggle about uncontrollably in the canoe. Climbing out on the quayside, I fling aside the paddle and tear into my skin with eight sharp fingernails.

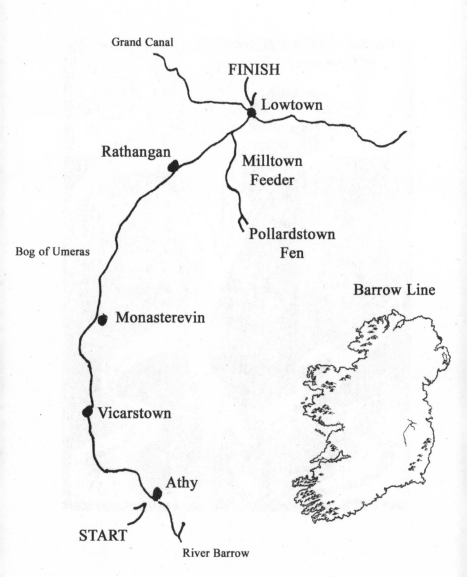

Grand Canal

FINISH

Lowtown

Rathangan

Milltown
Feeder

Bog of Umeras

Pollardstown
Fen

Barrow Line

Monasterevin

Vicarstown

Athy

START

River Barrow

upstream

The weather is in a fickle mood, and I am impatient to return to the water. On a humid afternoon I enter the canal at Athy and paddle upstream, just for a change – there is little current on this short stretch of waterway. The Barrow Line canal links Lowtown, on the Grand Canal, with Athy, on the River Barrow. The canoe is packed with camping gear, but only a limited supply of food and water, as I expect to find provisions in towns and villages along the way.

A minor road follows the canal for some distance, loose gravel raining down like hailstones whenever a car speeds by. Soon, the road diverges and I am alone at last. Before me stretches a long, lock-free section of waterway, sheltered and secluded. Far from anywhere, I pitch camp on the canal's grassy towpath. The fact that I have brought the wrong cylinder of gas for my stove, leaving me unable to boil water for tea or cook a hot meal, doesn't bother me too much. Tomorrow I will be able to refuel. Another addition to the camping gear is an inflatable mattress, which promises maximum comfort and a good night's sleep. An hour of heavy puffing brings it to life, but leaves me lightheaded and faint. By midnight I am wide awake and stone cold. The mattress must be to blame, providing zero insulation from the cold earth. I resolve to chuck it in the first available bin in the morning. In spite of pulling on every piece of spare clothing, I lie awake and shiver until dawn.

The sooner I return to the water, the quicker I'll warm up. By seven the following morning I am shoving away from the bank and energetically striking out towards Monasterevin. The canal passes through a verdant landscape of rolling pastures and handsome trees. The farther I progress, the denser the vegetation becomes, in the water and along the banks. A disembodied voice hails from the undergrowth.

'Hello, is somebody there?'

'Yes, I am here. I'm in a canoe,' I reply timidly.

After quick introductions, I learn that the stranger on the bank is Margaret Scully, a travel writer and broadcaster from Vicarstown. A long conversation ensues while we remain hidden to one another behind the high foliage. We discover we have much in common, both being keen travellers who prefer wandering off the beaten track. Margaret has recently made a documentary for radio about the Hare Krishna community on Lough Erne. We could probably talk all day, but Margaret's ancient collie dog is exhausted, and both turn for home. I paddle on, brimming with positivity after this rather surreal encounter, blissfully unaware of the misfortunes that lie in wait.

By now it feels as if I have wandered into a tributary of

the Amazon. The foliage is exotic and menacing, gunnera with leaves as large as umbrellas, Himalayan balsam that emits a distracting and slightly unpleasant smell, rushes with stems as thick as bamboo and floating fields of water lilies. After fifteen kilometres of strenuous paddling, I arrive below a lock on the outskirts of Monasterevin. I search in vain for an easy egress, but the banks are too steep and thick with brambles and nettles; the only option is to climb out at a very high jetty. 'Never stand up in a canoe.' I'm sure I read that advice somewhere, but apparently it didn't sink in. As soon as I stand, *Minnow* tosses me head first into the water and capsizes. My drybags, hat, coat, bailer and paddle drift about as I resurface, spluttering and disorientated in the middle of the canal. The canoe is brimful with muddy water, but, thankfully, it's still afloat.

'"Never stand up in a canoe." I'm sure I read that advice somewhere, but apparently it didn't sink in.'

My folding portage trolley has sunk out of sight. The canal is reasonably shallow, chest high, so I can at least stand up, and fortunately, it is bathtub warm. I do a quick health check to make sure I haven't severed any limbs, then slosh about trying to recover each piece of gear. The bank is too high for me to toss up the heavy drybags, a fact I accept only after several failed attempts. I'm forced to scramble in and out of the canal, hauling each item up on dry land. It's a frustrating and humiliating task thanks to the slippery mud and the weight of my waterlogged clothes. While I really could do with a little bit of help, I'm secretly relieved that no one is around to witness the embarrassing drama. Salvaging the canoe is an added challenge. The watertight bulkheads keep the hull afloat, but I still have to bail out litres of murky canal water before hauling it ashore. Lastly, I search the muddied waters for my phone, which I had carelessly tossed in the bottom of the canoe earlier that morning. It is lifeless – past the point of rescue – when I finally retrieve it. A deluge of monsoon-like proportions decides to bucket down. Given that I'm already sopping wet, there hardly seems any point in crawling under the hedge for shelter, so I sit shivering on the canalside, nursing a bruised ego and debating whether or not to continue.

Through gritted teeth and still-pouring rain, I decide to press on, portaging around the lock and re-entering the canal on its upper level. An aqueduct carries the canal across a dramatic ravine, over the River Barrow, which shimmers far below. The 12.35 Cork to Dublin express bugle-blasts as it hurtles over a viaduct. At the far side of the aqueduct is an impossibly low road bridge. There's a chance I'll make it underneath by lying flat in the bottom of the canoe. It's a tight squeeze as I hand-pull my way through; unnerving too, as cars and trucks rumble overhead. The plan had been to tie up and explore Monasterevin, and to fill my belly with hot tea and a breakfast roll or two, but I'm still drenched from the dunking and conscious of an evil smell coming from my shoes, so I paddle swiftly on.

The canal travels out across the Bog of Umeras. As a hot, gusty wind harries at my back, I hardly need to paddle the canoe; I just steer. Pike lurk beneath the surface of the gin-clear water. Every time I dip the blade, it makes contact with a fish. I can feel their muscular bodies bouncing off

the wooden paddle shaft. Most fresh-water fish avoid the midday sun, preferring to lurk in the cool shadows, but pike are different. Predatory and opportunistic, they lie just beneath the surface watching out for dragonflies and damselflies, which they snatch from the air in a single gulp.

A dozy horse spooked by my silent passage rolls its eyes, snorts and canter-farts up the towpath. The canal is dead straight as it cuts through the bog. The high vertical banks give the impression of a seemingly endless corridor, and I feel isolated from the outside world. The canal is choked with waterlilies, whose sinuous stems knot themselves around the paddle shaft. Reeds and bulrushes grow tall, thick and woody, encroaching right into the middle of the channel. Progress is frustratingly slow, and exhausting in the humid heat. It's a case of three strokes forward and two strokes back as I try to navigate a through passage. If it's difficult for me to make headway in a small canoe, it's hard to imagine a boat faring any better.

After several hours of tortuous paddling, my attention is drawn to a large glinting object on the horizon; it appears to be advancing along the canal. An engine thrums, punctuated by an ominous grinding metallic scream. It must be a boat, but its shape is odd, unlike any boat I've encountered before. Only when I see the gnashing blades do I realise it is a weedcutter, a primitive steel raft with a cutting bar mounted on the bow – a floating combine harvester, in other words. As the vessel pushes forward, the cutting bar chews its way through the reeds, ingesting the cut foliage and spewing a messy mulch in its wake. Frozen in mid-paddle, I wonder how on earth to navigate around the beast. A part of me wants to make an about-turn and flee back to Monasterevin. The skipper, clearly visible now in his boxy wheelhouse, has a determined set to his face. A pair of bright red mufflers covers his ears. He is focused on his task, and seems oblivious of my presence. At last, he makes eye contact and swerves the machine hard into the bank. For a moment I wonder if it is about to morph into an amphibious craft. The pilot signals me to carry on with a wave of his hand. I sidle past the gnashing blades and squeeze through the tiny space of clear water he has offered. I'm almost free when the boat's propeller churn catches the canoe broadside, hurling it into the bank. Seized with panic and convinced I am about to capsize again, I flail about in the reeds, forced to ditch the paddle and use my hands to pull the canoe free. At last, I get some traction, and with heart hammering wildly, I sprint for freedom. But the weed harvester is not finished with me. Glancing over my shoulder, I am horrified to see that the machine has turned and is now giving chase. I pound the water, furiously urging the canoe on faster, but the beast is in hot pursuit. My arms are as limp as overcooked spaghetti and my heart is about to explode as I career into Rathangan. Just beneath the lock gate I beach the canoe and collapse in a panting heap on the towpath. As the weedcutter churns past, I swear the driver throws me a wicked grin.

A deep rumble of thunder announces yet another downpour and I dive for cover inside my hastily pitched tent. Soggy-bottomed, I should use the opportunity to change into dry clothes, but I really can't be bothered. Instead, I stare through the mesh curtain as stair-rods beat off *Minnow*'s upturned hull, a big pout dragging down my face. The deluge passes and I set out along the towpath in search of the town centre. A worn path leads to a road that cul-de-sacs in an industrial estate. I know there's a town here somewhere, but in this warren of warehouses and factory units it is difficult to tell where. A sign in the distance

'Past the point of making rational decisions and teetering on the brink of defeat, I slouch back to camp.'

advertises Kentucky Fried Chicken. The sight of Colonel Sanders' smiling face has never looked more appealing. Thoughts of hot fried chicken and a warm drink put a spring in my step. But there is no fast food outlet; instead, I stand at the foot of a huge billboard near a sports pitch. I have been tricked, lured through a concrete desert by a mirage. Past the point of making rational decisions and teetering on the brink of defeat, I slouch back to camp.

I have company on the canal bank: a car has somehow gained access. A gang of six young men spill out and proceed to engage in a bout of bare-knuckle boxing. Anxious to avoid becoming the object of their attention, which is challenging when you happen to be dressed in canary-yellow waterproofs, I slink into the tent and hunker down on the cold, hard ground. A bruised apple is all that's left of my rations. I gouge out the mealy bits with a penknife and wash it down with tepid water. Wallowing on a sleepless sea, I ask myself, 'What sort of idiot heads off camping without first testing their equipment?' 'How did I manage to capsize the canoe?' 'Why was I so careless with my mobile phone?' The answers are all self-defeating. The voice of doubt takes charge. Clearly, I'm not cut out for this sort of adventure. Tomorrow, I'll pack it in, send out a Mayday call and resume life as an armchair traveller.

Rathangan's town centre is a few minutes' paddle upstream, as I discover the following morning. I leave the canoe at a slipway and follow my nose in search of food.

Wary about leaving the canoe and gear unattended for any length of time, I grab a takeaway coffee, hot breakfast roll and a shopping bag full of sugary supplies, and jog back to the canal. When I swerve to avoid a misplaced bin, the lid springs off my to-go cup, sloshing the contents down my front. With a stream of curses, I drop my supplies on a stone seat and wipe off the worst of the mess. Gathering up the shopping bags, I notice a plaque embedded in the wall behind the seat and move in to take a closer look at the inscription. It's a memorial plaque, and carved in bold black lettering is a dedication to Rathangan's most famous native, Maura Laverty. It's not often you come across public monuments celebrating Irish women, and I feel compelled to linger.

Maura Laverty was born in Rathangan in 1907. She was a woman of many talents, which I am pleased to see the curators of this memorial have seen fit to highlight. She was a celebrity chef, playwright, novelist, journalist, an agony aunt and the author of Ireland's first TV soap, Tolka Row. At the age of seventeen she followed the route of many young Irish Catholic girls, travelling to Spain to work as a governess. During her time there, she worked her way up to become a private secretary, followed by a period as a features writer for the Madrid newspaper El Debate, submitting articles and poems to journals back home. On her return to Ireland, she pursued a career in writing, publishing eight novels, ranging from children's stories to adult fiction. Her work was critically well received, nationally and internationally, winning her several literary awards. Three of her novels were banned in Ireland by the Censorship Board. The consequences of censorship would have had a disastrous impact on sales, jeopardising future publishing contracts and having a stifling effect on the writer's creative expression. To supplement her income, Maura diversified, hosting an agony aunt session on national radio and contributing articles to women's magazines. For *Woman's Life* magazine, she wrote under not one but three pen names, Mrs Wyse, Dr Garry Myers and Delia Dixon. But food was Maura's enduring passion, and in writing about it she excelled. Copies of *Flour Economy*, *Kind Cooking* and *Full and Plenty* were very successful, and additional print runs sold out. Even today these books are considered valuable collectors' items. Descriptions of food and cooking are woven throughout her novels, and the recipes in her cookbooks are frequently accompanied by witty anecdotes. Maura clearly delighted in tongue-in-cheek humour, as demonstrated in this exquisite piece on preparing poultry, from *Kind Cooking*:

> Wise women dress themselves to suit their age. Wise cooks dress poultry with the same discernment. It is both unbecoming and unnecessary to overdress spring chicken with elaborate cooking. Keep the beauty treatments and sophisticated styles for the middle-aged and elderly ones, and you'll be rewarded by seeing even the hardiest and scraggiest become soft and yielding and attractive.

Wolfing down my bacon and egg roll, I imagine Maura would have had some sharp words to say about my food choice, never mind the previous night's failed search for Kentucky Fried Chicken. Yet how apt that my path should intersect with this determined and feisty woman. I crumple up the greasy fast-food packaging and stuff it in the overflowing bin. A crow materialises and hops in to investigate the new deposit. With my nagging hunger temporarily satisfied, I find I have emerged from my melancholic gloom and feel the will to continue my quixotic adventure. Inspiration really can happen in unexpected places.

Lowtown, and the junction to the Grand Canal, is at the end of the Barrow Line, a short distance upstream. In between, there are three locks to portage around; fortunately, all are straightforward and free of drama. Before reaching the end of the line, there's a small detour I want to make. As I approach Lowtown, I keep an eye out for the junction to the Milltown Feeder, a narrow channel which will take me into a mysterious watery world known as the Pollardstown Fen. This is a place I've been keen to explore for quite some time, and what better way to do so than by canoe?

The Milltown Feeder branches off eastwards. In the distance is the Hill of Allen, the first piece of elevated landscape I have seen in the past few days. The flow of water against which I paddle is surprisingly strong. Arm, shoulder and leg muscles start to complain. The waterway skirts the base of the hill, or what remains of it; much of the mound has been quarried, leaving a gaping grey wound on its western slope. Through gaps in the reeds and trees I catch glimpses of the outside world. Chequered fields of wheat, barley and conifer plantations have replaced the ancient raised bogland. As the name of this man-made channel suggests, Milltown, the area, once sustained a

> 'It seems to me that the closer I come to the water's source, the greater the force that repels me.'

thriving milling industry that can be traced as far back as the early twelfth century. The gristmills were water-powered, tapping into the fen's seemingly endless supply. I paddle doggedly onwards, my thoughts preoccupied with man-altered landscapes. It seems to me that the closer I come to the water's source, the greater the force that repels me. Momentum slips to a snail's pace. It is unlikely I will make it to the fen before dark.

Daylight is fading when I approach the Hanged Man's Arch, a low road bridge that sits on the margins of the fen. A heavy coil of blue rope dangles from the bough of a sycamore in the middle of the channel. Evidently children use it to swing out across the water, but against the backdrop of this particular bridge all I see is a sinister noose. A chilling tale is connected with this portal that tells a story of lost love and a boatman's inconsolable grief. Suitably spooked, I drop back downstream and pitch the tent elsewhere.

The air is chilly but the water is lukewarm when I slide *Minnow* down the bank in the early morning. Bird calls pierce and carry clearly through the thin air – wren, duck, blackbird, heron, crow. The light is pale and diffused, scattered by the vaporous air that hovers over the fen. Pockets of will-o'-the-wisp drift and curl on the water surface. I feel a keen sense of anticipation about the day ahead; something special is about to be revealed. Early commuter traffic rumbles over the Hanged Man's Arch, a jarring reminder of just how much the urban world encroaches on this wilderness. As soon as I glide beneath the crooked bridge, I enter a very different place.

The water clarity is mesmerising. I have never seen such crystallinity. It is transparent to the point of invisibility. I stop repeatedly and stare down into the depths. When I do look up, I am entranced by the rich plant life that flourishes along the banks. Surely I have entered the Garden of Eden. The hemp agrimony is in its prime, top-heavy, candyfloss-pink blooms wobbling on long stems. The angelica is on steroids, towering at least two metres above the canoe. Purple loosestrife is rampant, and its narrow vertical fronds are the perfect complement to the frilly green mare's-tail. Weaving through these towering beauties is kingcup, ragged robin and bog pimpernel. At the intriguingly named 'Point of Gibraltar', the channel divides; only shallow draft vessels such as mine can continue on from here. The two ditches were dug in the late eighteenth century, and the water that filled them was channelled down the Milltown Feeder to supply the Grand Canal. I take the right fork and follow a narrow stream deeper and deeper into the heart of the fen.

Again, I am drawn down into the depths of an enchanting underwater world. The stream bed is lush and undulating, with thriving forests of oxygenating plants – hornwort, milfoil, bottle brush. In places, the luxuriant growth is punctuated with mysterious bald patches. Small areas of pale grey sediment are littered with what look to be bone-like remains. I'm not entirely wrong; it dawns on me that these must be tufa springs. The milk-white shards are the remains not of dead animals but of dead plants. They are sometimes referred to as petrifying springs, where deposits of calcium carbonate, present in the water, build up around the plants, turning them to stone. If I float above the spring, wait and watch, I can see bubbles and tiny intermittent jets of water escaping through the silt. In some places the activity is quite vigorous, as water percolates and pulses upwards from the ancient subterranean lake that lies beneath the fen.

Feeling dizzy and slightly overwhelmed, I need a moment to digest this otherworldly experience. Relaxing against the thwart, I am horrified to see a huge female raft spider poised right beside my hand; she is clasped around a bulrush stem. Her leg span is easily seven centimetres. Two bright-yellow stripes define each side of her dark-brown body. She is clearly on the defence, because strung across the stems behind her is the nursery web. Through the gossamer sac I see hundreds of wriggling babies ready to hatch out into the world. Even to a confirmed arachnophobe, which I am, it is a compelling vision. Very slowly, I release my hold of the stem and gently drift away.

St John's Well is the limit of navigation. At this stage the channel has reduced to little more than a stream. Bright-green cress and water mint tickle the belly of the canoe. Drinking from a natural watercourse is not something I would normally risk, but here its appearance is so pristine that temptation overwhelms. Cupping my hands, I scoop up the sparkling-clear water and drink deeply. Every fibre of my being tingles as the elixir permeates. The ancient Celts believed that springs were portals into Otherworlds, supernatural realms where youth, beauty, health and happiness were everlasting gifts. These magical kingdoms are known by various names, Tír na nÓg, 'the land of eternal youth', Mag Mell, 'the plain of delight', and Tír fo Thuinn, 'the land under the wave'. The *immram* tales describe journeys into these worlds where the hero encounters otherworldly beings. He is granted immortality and everlasting happiness

'The ancient Celts believed that springs were portals into Otherworlds, supernatural realms where youth, beauty, health and happiness were everlasting gifts.'

should he decide to stay, but if he attempts to leave, these magical gifts will be revoked and he will be mortal once again.

One man who dared to venture into this Otherworld was Tom Lawrence, an acoustic ecologist and sound artist. His album *Water Beetles of Pollardstown Fen* is a strange and wonderful journey into a secret underworld. Lawrence dipped a hydrophone into the fen's watery pools and streams, capturing a sonic environment orchestrated by tiny insects. His recordings unveil a mysterious symphonic realm of water boatmen, lesser water boatmen, great diving beetles, whirligig beetles, water beetles and water scorpions. The musical opus exposes a bizarre world of blips, pips, thrills, pulsating thumps, clicks, whirring, purrs, rumbles, sizzles and buzzes. The sounds were produced by a process called stridulation, an act that involves the insect rubbing a limb across a ridged surface on its body to produce a noise. In the case of some water bugs, a serrated edge on the front legs is rubbed against a ridge on the side of its head. Scientists recently discovered that the lesser water boatman is the loudest creature on earth, relative to its size, of course, producing a noise level of up to 99.2 decibels, the equivalent of a petrol-powered lawn mower.

To the human ear, at least to mine, the recordings equate to randomness produced by the mechanical world of revving chainsaws, idling outboard engines or intergalactic laser weaponry, but there is something absorbing and meditative about them too. The final track on Lawrence's album, 'Grand Canal Springs', showcases a thirteen-minute performance by a water scorpion in an aggressive mood. The recording artist described how he had placed a hydrophone close to the bug, which expressed its hostility by stridulating for nine hours. Few who venture into the Otherworld ever return, and sadly this was the case for Tom Lawrence, who met his untimely death while making field recordings nearby on the Hill of Allen.

Pollardstown Fen is known locally as the Yellow Marsh. Throughout the spring and summer there is a flush of yellow flowering plants – bog asphodel, orchids, flag irises, marshwort, Saint John's-wort and wild sunflower. The topography is a mosaic of environs characterised by tall reed beds, quaking mats, saw sedge and woodland. Water is everywhere, a constant element that seeps and oozes to varying degrees throughout the seasons. Overflowing springs trickle into thin streams that unite to form broader rills and channels. A raised boardwalk has been built across a corner of the fen in an effort to protect the fragile habitat from human footfall. I pull into the bank near the platform and set out to explore on foot. The months of June, July and August should see a flush of ethereal beauties, from the refined grass-of-Parnassus to the shy bog asphodel. I have read that this is the perfect place for orchid hunting, and there is a host of varieties I would like to see – marsh, helleborine, butterfly, fly, fragrant, common and twayblade.

Soothed by the sound of swishing grass, and distracted by the explosive pop of ripening bulrushes casting out their seeds into the warm, dry wind, I lose all sense of time, until a spaniel, off its leash, crashes through the undergrowth, leaps onto the walkway and shakes itself vigorously, issuing forth a fine shower of muddy droplets.

The complex waterscape is sanctuary to a richly varied avian community, the tall reed beds affording secrecy and protection for birds to breed and raise their young. Written in my notebook is a long list of birds spotted here previously by keen birders. There are the usual home birds – mute swan, mallard, teal, pheasant, little grebe, grey heron, water rail, moorhen, coot, snipe, wood pigeon, kingfisher, meadow pipit, dunnock, robin, song thrush, mistle thrush, blackbird, blackcap, goldcrest, wren, wheatear, magpie, jackdaw, rook, hooded crow, starling, house sparrow, chaffinch, redpoll, goldfinch, bullfinch, reed bunting and many varieties of tit. Curlew, long-eared owl, buzzard, kestrel, sparrowhawk and yellowhammer have also been spotted. There are transient guests such as cuckoo, swift, sand martin, house martin, swallow, whitethroat, sedge warbler, grasshopper warbler, willow warbler, chiffchaff, spotted flycatcher, redwing, fieldfare, shoveler, wigeon, tufted duck and golden plover. There are occasional visitors, including whooper swan, gadwall, pintail, red-legged partridge, glossy ibis, barn owl, whinchat, Savi's warbler, reed warbler, wood warbler and raven. The ones I really hope to see are the exciting lone hunters of the skies, marsh and/or hen harrier (though my untrained eye may not be able to tell the difference), peregrine falcon, merlin and osprey. I sit on a bench and wait for the birds, but none reveal themselves. Perhaps it's too windy, too humid, the wrong time of day, or maybe the loose dog scared them off. By the time I get ready to leave, the only species I have ticked off the list is a tiny reed bunting.

Pollardstown Fen is the only known site in Europe to support three rare and endangered species of the whorl snail: *Vertigo geyeri*, *Vertigo angustior* and *Vertigo moulinsiana*, to give them their Linnaean names. The whorl snail is microscopic, its shell length averaging a mere two millimetres. Calcium carbonate is necessary for the construction of the snail's shell, and the mineral-rich waters of the fen are conducive to its existence.

Some years ago, the tiny unassuming whorl snail became the centre of attention, garnering headline billing in the national media with the *Irish Independent* declaring in 2003: 'Long wait over as "snail pace" bypass finally opens to traffic'. The nature of the controversy saw the whorl snail being blamed for the delay in construction of a much-needed bypass for Kildare town. The town, which lies close to and south-west of the fen, was regarded as one of the worst traffic bottlenecks in the country in the 1980s. To relieve the congestion, a major bypass was proposed, a section of

'The nature of the controversy saw the whorl snail being blamed for the delay in construction of a much-needed bypass for Kildare town.'

which would cut through the Curragh Aquifer. To minimise interference with the local stud farms and racing stables, the motorway would be constructed below ground level, and to prevent it from flooding, an enormous drainage scheme was envisaged. While most were in agreement that a bypass was essential, there were many who expressed concern at the impact such drainage would have on the local environment. Conservation and environmental groups feared an upset in the delicate balance that enabled the Pollardstown Fen to support species such as the whorl snail, and the potential impact on the Grand Canal's water supply.

Planning was delayed following a review by the Office of Public Works, a government agency whose remit includes the appraisal of issues that may affect aspects of national heritage. The state body took issue with the local authority's environmental impact report on several grounds, and requested more detailed analysis and an exploration of options that could lessen the impact on groundwater supply. In 1998, An Taisce, the National Trust for Ireland, brought the matter to the attention of the European Commission. On foot of this complaint, the commission ordered that all work cease on the bypass pending further investigation. Following intense negotiations, an agreement was eventually achieved that required the placing of an impermeable liner along the section of the road that cut through the aquifer, in order to minimise changes in the groundwater level.

Twenty-one years after it had first been proposed, the Kildare bypass finally opened. From an initial estimate of €55 million, the final cost of the project came in at

€160 million. Today the Pollardstown Fen is included in protective legislation and conventions. It is a Special Area of Conservation, a National Heritage Area, a Statutory Nature Reserve, a Ramsar site – a wetland site designated to be of international importance – and a European Biogenetic Reserve.

I turn the canoe and drift downstream, preparing to leave the fen. Back at the Point of Gibraltar, my exit is blocked by a family of swans. The cob and cygnet are indifferent to my presence; preening and foraging keeps them occupied. The pen (female) has other ideas. I had heard rumours about this swan, the notorious guardian of the fen. Few have managed to slip by this 'keeper of the gates' without a chase. I have no choice but to push past, and hope that speed will give me the advantage. She swims straight for me, crouching low in the water, chest and wing feathers all puffed out. Hissing loudly, she radiates aggression. Her webbed feet propel her at alarming speed. Paddling like the clappers, I streak past her and career back down the Feeder to Milltown, never once looking over my shoulder.

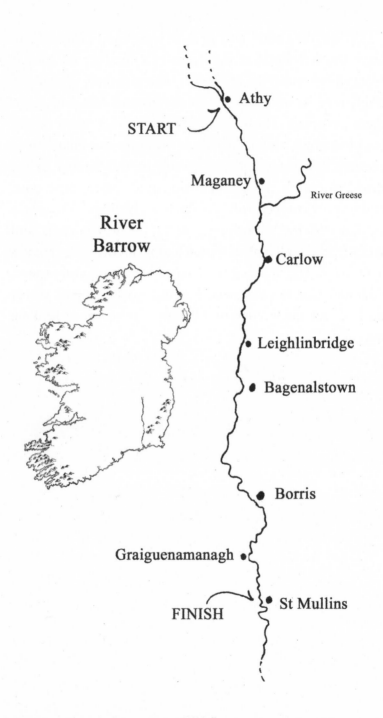

Athy

START

Maganey

River Greese

River
Barrow

Carlow

Leighlinbridge

Bagenalstown

Borris

Graiguenamanagh

FINISH

St Mullins

River Barrow

Shoppers form an orderly queue outside Athy's Aldi supermarket on the banks of the Barrow – the sight of so many people wearing face masks stops me in my tracks. It's the end of June, post-coronavirus lockdown, and we are all still adjusting to a dystopian world of social distancing, face coverings and other safety measures designed to combat COVID-19.

Almost a year has passed since I was last on the water, when I used the canoe to explore the Pollardstown Fen. My descent of the Barrow should have been completed months ago, but the virus and travel restrictions delayed that plan. As I set out on the water this morning, everything feels wobbly and unfamiliar. The confidence I achieved during previous adventures seems to have evaporated; my actions now are amateurish, hesitant and clumsy. As I hand-haul *Minnow* to the end of the slipway, her hull bumps off rough concrete, scratching paintwork. The bow noses out into the river and a sudden gust of wind catches the hull broadside, sending the canoe skittering downstream. Even the paddle feels awkward in my hands, probably because I'm holding it back to front and upside down. *Minnow* jigs and frisks in the open water. It feels as if I'm riding a fresh horse that wants to bolt across a field. I shuttle between the riverbanks trying to settle nerves and get a feel for the canoe once again. Finally, I turn the hull, point the bow downstream and submit to the river's pull.

The plan had been to descend the river in the company of a friend, Annabel. She's an adventurous, fit and hardy type, whom I knew would be a perfect kayaking and camping partner on this river journey. But Annabel's world was turned upside down when COVID-19 claimed the life of her husband, the film-maker Liam O'Neill. In a cruel twist of fate, Liam became infected with the virus on a hospital ward while attending a routine health check. The virus took hold and swept through his body, and after several weeks in intensive care he finally succumbed. Bereaved, Annabel and the couple's two children wrestled with despair. The rest of us, family and friends, stood at a distance on the sidelines, stunned into silence.

Apart from a few heartbreaking phone conversations, I had not seen Annabel for several weeks. She was in a dark, unreachable place, navigating her own Stygian river. Those of us who had survived the first wave were kicking to the surface, gasping for air as lockdown restrictions eased. My thoughts homed in on the River Barrow and the unfinished business of my inland waterways journey. Access to waterways had been outside my travel limit for the duration of lockdown, and I longed to get out on the water again and rekindle the spirit of adventure. A spell of fine weather coincided with an easing of travel restrictions – it was time to take on the river, even if it meant going without Annabel. Much as I enjoy paddling solo, embracing its challenges and the freedom of travelling at my own pace, I knew I couldn't manage the Barrow alone. The next best travelling companions, and the only people available at short notice, were my parents. Having shielded at home for months, they were eager for a change of scene and agreed to join me and help portage the canoe around the numerous locks. Their choice of transport was two vintage Raleigh bikes, my mother's a 'High Nelly' bought second-hand over forty years ago. Both bikes are sturdy black roadsters with upright frames, swept-back handlebars and wide leather saddles. Matching pedal to paddle, they planned to travel along the grassy towpath following the river's course.

As Ireland's second-longest river, the Barrow is 192 kilometres long, and flows unhindered from source to shining sea. Its true source is difficult to pin down. On the slopes of the Slieve Bloom mountains, water oozes from the heath as from a weeping sponge. Streams trickle and pool, gathering mass and momentum. In the foothills at Clamp Hole waterfall in County Laois the young river is formed. The weight of water tumbling down the rock hints at what's to come downstream. It takes a while for the river to assert itself as it meanders around the countryside, sometimes heading east, then north, eventually turning southwards. These headwaters are shallow and filled with unexpected hazards, too difficult to navigate even by canoe, but from Monasterevin, north of Athy, the river can be navigated all the way to Waterford and into the Irish Sea.

A brisk current speeds the canoe through the central arch of the town's main road bridge. Overhead, the busy main road is gridlocked with stationary traffic, harassed drivers twitching impatiently behind their steering wheels.

The cause of the blockage is a big, shiny, red tractor hauling a trailer-load of grain, taking up the width of the roadway. No such congestion for me; it's wide-open water and full steam ahead.

Earlier, walking through the town, I found myself standing beside a larger-than-life bronze statue of one of the world's greatest explorers, Sir Ernest Shackleton, a local hero, who was born not far from Athy. The monument is a relatively new addition to the town square, unveiled in 2016, according to an adjacent plaque. With arms folded across his chest and feet braced against the uneven ice, he cuts a commanding presence, despite the shapeless polar garments. Finding it impossible to resist, I visited the town's museum and lost myself in Shackleton's world.

The Heroic Age of Antarctic Exploration began at the end of the nineteenth century, and Shackleton's polar exploits during that era are legendary. In his lifetime, he made three attempts to reach the South Pole, and, despite coming within a hair's breadth, the goal was never realised. But Shackleton's fame is not defined by his failure; his reputation was built on a model of outstanding leadership skills, courage and resilience. The *Endurance* expedition of 1914 exemplified these skills. The mission of the Shackleton-led team was to cross the Antarctic via the South Pole. Icebound and shipwrecked, the crew was forced to abandon their ship, *Endurance*, trekking for weeks

'But Shackleton's fame is not defined by his failure; his reputation was built on a model of outstanding leadership skills, courage and resilience.'

on drifting ice flows. They reached Elephant Island, from where Shackleton and five of the crew sailed and rowed one of the three small open lifeboats across the Southern Ocean in a heroic quest for survival. Miraculously, all twenty-eight men survived to tell the tale. In a flurry of poetic prose, Shackleton wrote:

> We had pierced the veneer of outside things. We had suffered, starved, and triumphed, grovelled down yet grasped at glory, grown bigger in the bigness of the whole. We had seen God in his splendors, heard the text that Nature renders. We had reached the naked soul of man.

A century later and this spellbinding story is still relevant, and has spurred a renaissance. Students at Harvard Business School have been introduced to the epic voyage, analysing it in the context of Shackleton's leadership skills and how he managed to sustain morale, loyalty and commitment in his team. As countries around the world grapple with the unfolding crisis brought on by the COVID pandemic, researchers have turned again to Shackleton and his lessons in crisis leadership.

But back to the water. The river whisks me past a dizzying time-lapse of Athy's architectural heritage, looming medieval ramparts, Georgian façades and the revolutionary community library – a former church building constructed in the 'Brutalist' style. The warm sunshine and the weightless buoyancy speed me towards euphoria. My mood soars like a bird rising on a thermal current of air. The canoe skims past the junction to the Barrow Line canal. Memories of my previous canal voyage fizz to the surface: the humiliating capsize, the bare-knuckle boxers, fast-food hallucinations and the otherworldly environment of Pollardstown Fen. But there's no time to reminisce. There's a weir straight ahead, and the river has intentions of dragging the canoe straight over the falls.

'Keep close to the bank,' shouts my father, who has materialised beside me on the towpath, wheeling along on his bike. The weir curves in a wide arch out from the opposite shore. The pull is surprisingly strong, and the roaring falls overwhelm all other sound as I skirt along its lip. Most canoeists shoot the weirs, since the falls are at a gentle incline and the drop is never more than two metres. It's a fun experience that comes with a small adrenaline rush, and it's the easiest way to avoid the challenging lock portages. If I was paddling a robust fibreglass canoe, I would happily choose this option, but *Minnow* isn't built for weirs; her thin plywood hull would splinter on the hidden rocks and boulders. I researched the possibility of 'lining' the canoe over the weirs – attaching a long rope to the stern and feeding the hull over the falls – but this seemed an equally risky business, destined to end in tears. It was back to my nemesis, portaging, for the time being.

Safely past the weir, I peel away from the river and guide the canoe into a lateral canal towards Ardreigh, the first river lock. The still water is treacle-thick, overgrown and dense with weeds. Within minutes I'm huffing and puffing through a tangle of slippery water lily stems and trailing long fronds of pondweed. At the entrance to the lock, I meet an early challenge – how to climb ashore? Squinting up at the 'cyclers' standing silhouetted high above on the quayside, I realise I haven't a hope of scaling the wall, and am forced to retrace my way back up the canal in search of an easier egress. Where the bank is slightly lower, I scramble ashore, strong-armed up by my father. Between the two of us we carry the canoe along the towpath and around the lock, while my mother fetches and carries my gear. With twenty-one more locks ahead, clearly this is going to be a slow journey, requiring no small team effort! Sobered by the experience, we decide to raid the picnic panniers, tucking into flapjacks washed down by scalding mugs of whiskey-laced coffee. Then it's off to rejoin the river just below the lock, a challenge as we hack a way through nettles and cling perilously to clumps of weeds. It will be a miracle if I survive the journey without a few dunkings.

The river is in sparkling form – energised from tumbling over the weir and rapids. Its surface is littered with blobs of foam that spin like whirling dervishes in the fast-flowing current. The canoe joins the flow and is whisked along at warp speed – at least it feels that way to me. For a time, I manage to keep up with the cyclers, who are travelling at full tilt on the towpath. As the channel widens and deepens, the river relaxes. When I look up, they have disappeared, leaving me alone on the water. I rest the paddle across the gunnels and let the canoe drift. This is the release I've been craving, and I want to savour it. The past few months have seen us all trapped on a roller-coaster ride of anxiety, fear, sadness and frustration. Locked down at home, it was impossible to avoid the wall-to-wall media coverage of the unfolding pandemic. The constant narrative ground you down and set your nerves on edge. Now, out here on the river, I feel as though I have slipped that world and entered a parallel universe – a far brighter world charged with optimism and wonder.

'Now, out here on the river, I feel as though I have slipped that world and entered a parallel universe – a far brighter world charged with optimism and wonder.'

A sudden flash from the bank, a tiny fireball of gas-flame blue, streaks across *Minnow*'s bow. Taken by surprise with a gasped intake of breath and paddle frozen in mid-air, I follow the bird's hurried flight path. There was a time when I kept a headcount of every kingfisher I saw, but somewhere, back along the Grand Canal, I gave up when they became a commonplace occurrence. This is my closest encounter yet, almost a collision. The bird was equally surprised; startled in flight, it fluttered briefly, banked sharply, collected itself and fled crying downriver. In the breathtaking moment as it tumbled over the canoe, I experienced its kaleidoscopic colours, from the burnt orange of its breast to the iridescent blues of its back and wing feathers.

An old proverb says that only the righteous see the kingfisher. Being neither good, virtuous nor innocent, I'm not sure how I managed to slip through the net. My luck with seeing kingfishers is more than likely due to travelling by canoe, slowly, soundlessly and at water level. I know people who walk the canal and riverbanks for weeks without ever sighting

'An old proverb says that only the righteous see the kingfisher.'

one. Most birds are identified and located first by their call or song, but the kingfisher is unusually quiet. Unlike other birds, it does not announce its presence. All it has is a flight call, a high-pitched note like a squeaky wheelbarrow wheel. Its under-body colouring blends in subtly with the riparian vegetation. Several times while paddling along, I've stared right at a kingfisher perched in the reeds and not noticed it until it erupts into flight, revealing the unmistakable high-octane blue feathering. Blue is an unusual colour in the animal kingdom. Most vertebrates are unable to produce blue pigment. The blue of the kingfisher is caused not by pigment (its feathers are actually brown) but by structural coloration, the result of light falling on and reflecting off transparent layers of feather cells. This similar iridescent trait is shared by peacocks, birds of paradise and even magpies.

The high vertical banks along the Barrow provide the perfect sites for the kingfishers to excavate their burrows. For creatures so exotic and stunning, I was surprised to learn that they have the worst housekeeping skills in the animal kingdom. Apparently, their burrows are pretty squalid, littered with droppings and food waste. The canalised stretches along the river are prime real estate for the kingfisher, clear and shallow, with slow-moving water. Overhanging branches serve as lookout points, and there is an abundance of food, including minnows, sticklebacks, tadpoles and dragonflies.

The kingfisher is known in Ireland by several other names – some call it the *cruidín*, meaning the 'little hunchback', and others refer to it as *biorra an uisce*, a 'water spear'. In the realm of biomimicry – finding clues in nature

to help solve complex human problems – the kingfisher
as 'water spear' has played a key role. For example, by
the late 1990s, Japanese engineers had pioneered high-
speed bullet trains capable of travelling at 300 kilometres
an hour. However, the bullet-shaped nose of the driver's
cabin was proving problematic; when passing through a

tunnel, a cushion of air built up at the head of the train, which exploded with a sonic boom at the moment of exit. Residents living in the vicinity of the rail line complained about the disruption, and called for a solution. It was to the kingfisher that the engineers turned for inspiration. The story goes that one of the team's engineers, a keen 'birder', had witnessed the manner in which a kingfisher dives with minimal water disturbance. The key to its success is the size and design of its bill. Wedge-shaped and making up a third of the bird's length, the bill allows the kingfisher to penetrate the water surface with speed and stealth as it targets its prey beneath. The same principles were adapted to improve the aerodynamics of the Shinkansen (bullet train), thus reducing air resistance. Not only did it solve the problem of sonic booms, the new streamlined design resulted in trains travelling 10 per cent faster, and with 15 per cent greater energy efficiency.

Onwards I paddle. Another weir ahead, this one stretching downriver for well over a hundred metres. An ash tree, felled in a flood, has snagged on the weir's lip, brightly coloured plastic waste tangled in its branches. A family of mute swans stands on the rim. Too busy preening, they show no interest in my presence. I steer away from the river and wade down another weed-choked canal to Levitstown lock, where the cyclers are waiting.

The picnic panniers are raided again. Our plates are heaped high with gourmet fare, worlds apart from the meagre rations of my previous voyages. We sit in a row on the lock gate's outstretched arm, a single shaft of wood hewn from a giant tree. After several hours on the water, we have yet to meet a boat, cyclist or walker. It feels as if we have trespassed onto private property. The portage and relaunch are a repeat performance of the first lock, with a hint of tetchiness creeping in, thanks to stinging nettles and hooking briars.

Late in the afternoon, the sinking sun casts long shadows across the water. We have travelled almost twenty kilometres and my arms and back are starting to complain. At Maganey lock the cyclers decide to call it a day and set off on their return journey to Athy. We'll meet again tomorrow farther downstream. I continue on alone, scouting for a place to pitch the tent along the riverbank. There are no official campsites along the Barrow, but wild camping is allowed, provided you don't obstruct the towpath. Carlow is a short distance downstream and I'm anxious to find a place outside the suburbs. When it comes to solo camping, there is a fine balance between solitude and safety, especially for women. Camping too close to urban settings invariably attracts unwelcome attention, especially night-time visitors. Anywhere that's accessible to cars is to be avoided. Since the Barrow passes through several towns and the towpath is frequently used by walkers and cyclists, finding a safe place to camp is going to be challenging. Bestfield lock lies just ahead, and is the last lock before Carlow. In theory, it should be the perfect layover, with plenty of flat, grassy space for the tent, but rumour has it that the lock is haunted. Boatmen speak of mysterious tapping sounds on their boat hulls when moored there overnight. I hastily scrap the idea of staying there, having no wish to add ghosts to my long list of anxieties. Instead, I choose a quiet stretch of riverbank, where the little River Greese joins the main flow. There's just enough room away from the towpath to pitch the tent and stow the canoe out of harm's way.

For a while, as I fumble around with tent pegs and guy ropes, I'm jumpy and wary, constantly looking over my shoulder or straining to make out a sound. The dull routine of housebound life is kicked aside and dormant senses have been triggered. In this strange environment the mind scrambles to process new sounds, sights and smells. A one-pot meal cooked on the unsteady stove serves to distract and relax me. Shelter and food, two vital needs, ticked off the list. If the experience of solo camping is so stressful, why do I put myself through it? It's a question I'm never fully able to explain. Four walls and a roof are perfectly fine, but wild camping makes me feel alert and alive, nervous yes, but alert and alive. Some sort of feral genes must be embedded in my DNA. The evening is quiet and uneventful – no spectacular sunset or glorious bird song, just a subtle transition of day into night. The distant hum of road traffic gradually fades away. Hungry midge clouds begin to gather and drift. I zip the tent door closed behind me and burrow into the duck-down sleeping bag. Sleep never comes easily on the first night of camping, no matter how tired I feel.

I'm wide awake, snug, waiting for dawn to break. Heavy dewdrops streak rivulets down the canvas walls. A wood pigeon clears its airwaves, finds its rhythm and

'Four walls and a roof are perfectly fine, but wild camping makes me feel alert and alive, nervous yes, but alert and alive.'

coos the same tune over and over. Small birds join the choir: blackbirds, a robin, thrushes and a wren. A hooded crow squawks, like an unwelcome heckler. Four thirty, five o'clock, sometime after six I worm out of the sleeping bag, unzip the door and flood the interior chamber with cold, damp air. Camp living has to be relearned. I've become too domesticated over the past few months. The saucepan of water takes an eternity to boil over the spitting gas flame. Breakfast is muesli soaked in boiling water, unsavoury yet essential fuel. While packing up camp, I realise I've got the sequencing of items all wrong; everything has to be unpacked. I engage in a humiliating wrestle with the sleeping bag, which refuses to return to its compression sack. I'm ready at last to slide with the canoe back into the cold river water. The plan for the day is to continue the short stretch downstream, and to meet the cyclers in the centre of Carlow town sometime before midday. This morning I'm free to paddle at my own pace. There is time simply to drift and let the flow carry the canoe gently along – time to observe and listen.

'There is time simply to drift and let the flow carry the canoe gently along – time to observe and listen.'

Since leaving Athy, the river has traced a relatively straight journey south. The two banks – the east bank forming the border of County Kildare, while the west bank represents the edge of County Laois – feel worlds apart. The Kildare side is stately and ordered; hedges are trimmed and the towpath is lightly mown. Because the outside world is screened off, my field of vision is concentrated on immediate surroundings. The eye slowly attunes to fine details, homing in on individual flowers that form a continuous herbaceous border along the riverbank: orchids, yarrow, clover, mare's-tail, plantain, willow herb, geranium, mallow, celandine. Hogweed, Himalayan balsam, hoarhound, thistle, nettle and bramble wrestle to dominate the scene.

By comparison, Laois's bank is wild and dense, with bushy alder and silvery willows sweeping the water, and iris and lilies competing for light and space. Waterfowl nesting in the bank dart in and out of this dark and secretive world. Sometimes, through a break in the trees, I'll snatch a glimpse of the outside world and crane my neck to see what I might be missing. But the views are mostly disappointing: field after field of intensively farmed cropland, uninspiring and lacking in diversity. Everything that interests me is right here on the river. Suddenly, on a bend, the soothing green leafiness evaporates and light spills in like a dramatic lifting of the blinds. I am taken by surprise. A post-industrial wasteland with footprints of warehouses and a towering chimney is all that remains of an enormous sugar refinery, once the jewel in Carlow's commercial crown.

Carlow has shaped itself around the river, its evolution a familiar story shared by many other river towns, like Enniskillen on the Erne and Athlone on the Shannon. It starts with a strategic crossing point, followed by a fortified castle, around which a town grows to service people's needs. In Carlow's case, multi-storey mills tapped into the navigation highway, so that warehouses and quays expanded along the banks. Today, where the river passes through the town, a public park fills the space once occupied by trade and industry. The green space was developed over a decade ago as part of a plan to regenerate the waterfront. Before the redevelopment, surveyors branded the waterfront as 'informal and organic', a polite way of describing a general state of neglect. Lofty ideals were proposed to encourage greater interaction with the river and inspire redevelopment. Bulldozers moved in and cleared the five-hectare site, which for decades had festered as a landfill site. The result is a wide public space, planted and furnished, with steps leading down to the water's edge. As I approach the slipway, a welcoming party of juvenile mute swans swims over to investigate. Bachelors – at least fifty of them – surround the canoe. When they finally accept that I haven't come bearing the promised bag of stale bread crusts, they lose interest and swim off.

Reunited with the cyclers, I continue my journey downriver, carrying the canoe around several locks and escaping the town's suburbs. The river, all muscle now, ploughs a deep, straight furrow through a broad and fertile valley. Fields of wheat and barley ripple in the warm breeze. The current is strong and fast, pulling the canoe along determinedly. Even if I wanted to stop, I couldn't; whereas yesterday I could sit and drift, today I'm just about in control. The locks keep coming. A signpost points to the entrance of Milford canal, which I would certainly have missed, so completely overgrown has it become. The canoe slows to a halt as it surfs

'The river, all muscle now, ploughs a deep, straight furrow through a broad and fertile valley.'

onto a bed of thick weed – this is barely a ditch, never mind a canal. Paddling through the vegetation is farcical and exhausting.

It is hard to imagine that this waterway was once a busy thoroughfare. At its peak, 89,000 tonnes of heavy goods were carried annually by barges travelling between Dublin, Athy and all the way down to the tidal ports of New Ross and Waterford. The figure equates to roughly 1,800 barge movements, and such a volume of traffic ensured a clear and navigable waterway, particularly along the lateral canals. Nowadays, you might be lucky to count on one hand the number of boats passing by on a single day during the summer months.

Traces of this river's industrial past are still very much in evidence – huge mills and maltings, warehouses, harbours and boatyards. When it came to pass that livelihoods were no longer dependent on the river and commercial traffic dwindled, the navigation entered a period of decline. At first the state of dereliction bothered me. The sight of all the abandoned lock-keeper's cottages, the roofless mills, the pigeon-infested warehouses and overgrown canals saddened and disappointed me. It was only when browsing through old photographs of the Barrow that I realised how little has changed on the river in well over a century. For some reason there was never any rush to bulldoze and redevelop; everything remains just as it was. The Barrow is a place suspended in time, and therein lies part of its charm.

A black-and-white photograph has a timelessness of its

'The Barrow is a place suspended in time, and therein lies part of its charm.'

own. Remove the colour from a scene and you reduce the number of visual clues as to when the image was taken. On my desk at home is a copy of *Jane W. Shackleton's Ireland*, the pages of which are filled with poignant black-and-white photographs recording Irish life from the late 1800s. The images were made by the Irish-born photographer Jane W. Shackleton, cousin-in-law to Ernest Shackleton. In 1893, Jane travelled along the River Barrow photographing what she saw. Several of the images have been reproduced in the book that bears her name. Looking through them now, I am struck by how recognisable the riverscape remains. The mills, the locks, bridges and quays look the same today as they did for Jane.

Her images of the Barrow are part of a much larger body of work documenting Ireland's inland waterways. In 1894 she travelled along the Grand Canal, recording scenes of turf-loading, dredging, bargemen and the smouldering brick kilns at Pollagh. Other adventures took her along the River Shannon, stopping off at many of the places that I too visited – Clonfert, Banagher, Clonmacnoise and Inchcleraun on Lough Ree.

Jane's mode of transport was a twenty-seven-foot motor launch that she and her husband, Joseph Shackleton, commissioned. The *Pearl*, a slim, wooden-hulled vessel, appears in several of her photographic studies. It had a low, open-ended forward cabin, providing just enough shelter from the rain, and there was seating in the central sunken cockpit and on cushions around the stern deck. A large blue ensign fluttered on a flagpole attached to the stern. The vessel was powered by a tiny three-horsepower engine. Jane took her camera on their waterway adventures, recording canal and riverbank scenes, encounters with individuals engaged in daily life and wild camping expeditions on deserted islands.

When Jane took up her camera in the 1880s, photography was still a relatively new invention. The cameras used then were cumbersome wooden boxes with extendable leather bellows and heavy brass lenses, all mounted on a primitive wooden tripod. The latent images were fixed on delicate sheets of glass. A single glass plate was used for each photograph, to be developed later, using a cocktail of chemicals in a darkroom, a process Jane had mastered. Composing an image with a view camera takes time and a lot of patience – for several years I used similar equipment and processes in my own artwork. In order to study the image on the ground-glass screen, the photographer must disappear underneath a dark cloth, blocking out as much ambient light as possible. The photographer views the image presented upside down and back to front.

Jane's studies were not just confined to the Irish waterways; they extended well beyond. The Aran Islands, in particular, captured her interest, causing her to visit the islands with her camera on nine occasions. As an elected member of the Royal Society of Antiquaries, she contributed many images to the society's photographic collection of antiquities – monuments of archaeological interest and local architecture. There were journeys overseas too, exploring European countries and farther afield. As her confidence behind the camera grew, Jane's photographic style tended towards the documentary, and it is this approach that sets her apart from other photographers of that era. Her studies of the working classes and rural and island communities are honest and unflinching. It's impossible to avoid the pervading sense of hardship and poverty expressed in many images. Jane's photographs present us with a rare glimpse of an Ireland transitioning through the late Victorian and Edwardian eras. Her photographs serve as important visual references of society, place and time at a pivotal point in Ireland's history.

We are coming to the end of a productive day on the water. Another personal best has been achieved: twenty-four kilometres and five lock portages. (A competitive streak lurks inside me that is always keeping tabs.) The cyclers turn and disappear back up the towpath to Carlow, leaving me alone on the river. I slip unseen through the village of Leighlinbridge, pulled inexorably by the river towards another weir, and hunt for the entrance to the lateral canal. Another weed-choked channel, little more than the paddle's width, is camouflaged in the riverbank. A short way in and I'm regretting having entered. Every stroke of the paddle ends up knotted in thick, stringy weed. With patience running thin, I find the first available place to leave the water and collapse on the riverbank. Tonight's unscheduled camp is on the long and narrow island that separates the river from the canal, in a lumpy cow's meadow that's out of sight of prying eyes. When the breeze stops, the midges come out in their droves, forcing me into the tent despite the long, bright evening.

The following morning I'm back on the water, stiff-limbed, groggy and loitering around the boat slipway at Bagenalstown waiting for the cyclers. An attempted landing has been thwarted by a gaggle of belligerent geese. In the shadows of Rudkin's Mill I drift the canoe and wait. Every mill along the Barrow tells a story, but this one in particular caught my attention. It's one of the oldest mills on the river, built in 1690. The Rudkin family sold the property and emigrated to America in the eighteenth century. There the family's milling interests took an interesting turn. In 1937 Henry Rudkin, a Wall Street stockbroker, married Margaret Fogarty, the daughter of Irish emigrants. Because of their son's special dietary needs, Margaret began experimenting in her kitchen to make a palatable gluten-free bread. After several failed attempts she eventually had spectacular success. News of her delicious bread grew, and soon she was taking orders from specialty health food stores. As demand for the product increased, Margaret was obliged to move her baking operation out of her home kitchen and into larger, purpose-built premises. The business continued to expand, branching out into frozen produce, biscuits, crackers and pastry, under the company name 'Pepperidge Farm'. These days the company has an annual turnover in excess of a billion dollars.

As soon as the cyclers arrive and strap on the panniers bulging with the all-important picnic hamper, we set off downstream. My father has brought a windlass (lock key) with him today, and has it strapped to the crossbar of his Raleigh. Instead of portaging, we're going to try to descend the river by travelling through the locks. All the locks on the Barrow are manually operated, and a windlass is needed to raise and lower the sluice gates. I've tried this only once before, on the Grand Canal, and the amount of persuasion it took is still fresh in my mind.

The lock chamber is full and the gates are open to receive me. I take a deep breath as the heavy gates heave shut behind me. My father raises the sluices at the opposite end of the chamber and the water level around me slowly begins to sink. All the locks on the Barrow are deep but this one is the deepest, sinking down by well over three metres. Behind me the wooden gates creak and groan against the weight of the water. There is no escape ladder out of the enclosed space; if I get into trouble, the only prop is a heavy chain that dangles down the chamber wall, to which I cling resolutely. After what feels like an eternity, the water level inside equalises with the lower canal, and the gates creak open. I paddle out into dazzling sunshine and rejoin the surging river.

Paddling away from Bagenalstown, we enter an Arcadian landscape, a gently undulating countryside sweeping down to the foothills of the Blackstairs Mountains. Rich and fertile pasture land is filled with glossy herds of bloodstock, swishing their tails at flies. Elderflower blooms along the towpath, its sweet, heavy scent carried with the breeze. The locks slide by and I don't have to lift a finger – Fenniscourt, Slyguff, Ballyellen. My parents are doing all the heavy work, opening and closing the gates, raising and lowering the sluices. Day three on the water and we have still to meet another boat or human being.

Towards the end of a long, hot summer's day, we arrive at Ballytiglea and break open another thermos of tea. My parents reminisce about their first boat trip along the Barrow, a honeymoon voyage forty-odd years ago. The locks and canals were in such a sorry state back then that their boat could go no farther than this point. It's a sweet

'My parents reminisce about their first boat trip along the Barrow, a honeymoon voyage forty-odd years ago.'

spot on the river, hidden away from roads and towns. We part company, my parents pedalling back along the towpath to fetch their car, while I float on downstream. Now the river passes through a small wooded glen. Oak trees, towering and majestic, shroud the gentle slopes down to the riverside. A buzzard, drifting above the canopy, silhouetted against the pale evening sky above the river, issues a lonesome piercing cry.

This part of the Barrow is familiar territory to me. It was from here that I hired an open canoe for a one-day river cruise, a joyful ride that inspired this, my present adventure. In a sense I have come full circle on my epic canoe journey. I glide past the weir, basking in its rapturous applause, and pull out on the towpath at Borris lock. My home is a stone's throw away, but I'm not remotely tempted; I want to camp beside the river one last time.

The air is cool and the ground damp in the little patch of garden in front of the old lock-keeper's cottage. The tent pegs sink into the soft earth. The ground along the towpath is usually so heavily compacted that it causes the metal pegs to buckle, or resists them altogether. I set up the gas stove and boil a saucepan of water for tea.

Camping in woodland makes for a refreshing change. The sounds, the light, the sights and smells are all new to me. The tiny sliver of an island that separates river from canal supports five healthy plum trees weighted down with fruit. The woods are part of Borris House demesne, and are well maintained. Recently cleared of invasive laurel, the trees have space to breathe and shape themselves. The great estate is the ancestral home of the MacMurrough Kavanaghs, a family of ancient dynasty. As direct descendants of the Mac Murchadha, kings of Leinster, they controlled over 30,000 acres of land. Today, Borris House and estate extends over 500 hectares, and it remains within the family; its current custodians are Morgan and Sara MacMurrough Kavanagh.

'The great estate is the ancestral home of the MacMurrough Kavanaghs, a family of ancient dynasty.'

The raucous throaty croak of a pheasant startles me awake. It takes a moment to get my bearings. It's still pitch dark in and outside the tent – extra dark because of the trees. It's too early to rise just yet. More pheasants, calling and returning, staking out their territory for everyone to hear. Thousands of them strut around these woods, bred as hunting quarry for the winter shooting season. The dawn chorus gets off to a slow start, dominated at first by pigeons, then jackdaws and some miserable squawking hooded crows. Thrushes, blackbirds and robins fall into tune. I kick off the sleeping bag and crawl on all fours through the tent door. Outside it's chilly and damp. Black shapes slowly take on colour. I set a saucepan of water to boil and begin packing up my things for the last leg of this voyage. Somewhere nearby, a woodpecker hammers out a Morse code signal. A jay swoops past with a blood-curdling screech. By the time I have the camp dismantled, folded and stowed, the chorus has subsided, and only pigeons remain to fill the void.

I slide the canoe into the water below the lock, drop

in my gear and shimmy gracelessly down a pillar into the open hull. All is quiet on the river. I could be a thousand miles from anywhere, or the last person on earth. For centuries it was frowned upon for a woman to travel alone. Those who felt inclined to make a journey beyond their home place could do so only in the company of a chaperone or husband. The catalogue of risks implicit to women constrained their opportunities to travel extensively and bravely. Historically, expedition travel was regarded as far too physically demanding for women, and lacking creature comforts. Happily, it is now taken for granted that women are as capable as men when it comes to physically challenging expeditions, and have no need for pampering along the way. However, the fear of assault and harassment remains.

'All is quiet on the river. I could be a thousand miles from anywhere, or the last person on earth.'

The early women travellers tended to be rich, white and members of the upper class – Gertrude Bell, Beryl Markham, Vita Sackville-West, to name a few. Add to this list a person of Irish interest, Lady Harriet Kavanagh of Borris House, whose exploits have only recently come to light. It was a thrill to discover that such a person existed on my own doorstep. Lady Harriet was passionate about travel, traversing much of continental Europe and exploring Africa and the Middle East. She is thought to be one of the first known Irish female travellers to Egypt. Born into a family of wealth and privilege, as the daughter of an ambassador she had the opportunity to travel throughout

Europe in the early nineteenth century. Following an arranged marriage to Thomas Kavanagh in 1825, Harriet moved into Borris House. In spite of her husband's ill health – he suffered from chronic gout – the family enjoyed several European adventures. Practical, pragmatic and resourceful, she took charge of all travel arrangements, booking accommodation, hiring transport and paying bills. On a day trip to Mount Vesuvius, she arranged for her invalided husband to be carried up the volcano in a chair so that he could accompany her.

Becoming a widow at the age of thirty-eight did not curb Lady Harriet's spirit of adventure. If anything, it spurred her on to embark on longer and more challenging escapades. In the early 1840s she set out for Egypt with three of her children in tow. In Cairo she hired two *dahabiyas*, traditional river sailboats: one for the boys, their tutor and the party's dogs; the other for herself and her daughter Hoddy. Departing Cairo, the party sailed up the Nile as far as Sudan. In the course of the voyage, their boats were overcome with an infestation of rats. Undeterred, Harriet instructed the boats to pull into a small riverside town and walked into the market, where she bought three cats. The cats were released on board but failed to do their job. The rat problem persisted. 'The rats have become so exceedingly troublesome that it became necessary, in order to get rid of them, to sink the boats,' wrote Harriet in her diary. The boats were refloated and the family continued their voyage.

After their Nile River adventure, Harriet decided to follow the route of the Israelites, crossing the Sinai desert to arrive in Palestine. It was a route that only three

European parties had ever attempted successfully. At no time did she consider what she was doing to be out of the ordinary. After thirty-six days in the desert, which they traversed by camel and on foot, the entourage arrived at St Catherine's Monastery on Mount Sinai. From there, the intrepid family unit visited Hebron, Bethlehem, Jericho and Jerusalem, and travelled farther afield to Jordan, Syria and the Lebanon.

Architecture and antiquities were what interested Harriet most on her travels. Days were spent visiting churches, palaces, tombs and ruins. In the course of her Egyptian and Middle Eastern travels, Harriet amassed a collection of artefacts and curios. Upon her death, the Royal Society of Antiquities of Ireland received these objects, and, in turn, loaned the collection to the National Museum of Ireland, where several pieces are displayed permanently.

In addition to writing her diaries, Harriet painted and sketched as she travelled. What her journal entries lack in rich descriptive detail, her sketchbooks and watercolours more than make up for. In the words of her niece, Mrs Steele, Harriet was a 'woman of high culture and of unusual artistic power ... her sketches and watercolour drawings assisted the records of her graphic pen in reproducing for the benefit of those left behind the beauties of the scenery in which she delighted'.

One of Lady Harriet's lasting legacies is the Borris Lace industry. Lace was a fashionable textile in Victorian times, and Irish lace was a highly regarded and sought-after commodity. Borris Lace was established as a famine-relief project by Harriet in 1846, with the aim of providing local women with a means of income support. Similar schemes were initiated on other landed estates in an attempt to alleviate the devastating hardship of the Famine. Harriet drew the designs for the Borris Lace patterns, and instructed the women how to make them. She then used her wealthy connections to market the finished product in Ireland, England and America. Borris Lace gained a reputation for its beautiful designs and fine crafting. This cottage industry, which occupied the female members of a household, was a vital financial lifeline for local villagers and estate tenants at a time of extreme hardship. Management of the enterprise was passed down to successive mistresses of the estate, until it was eventually wound up. In recent years, Borris lace-making has experienced a revival, thanks to a group of enthusiastic local craft workers.

'In recent years, Borris lace-making has experienced a revival, thanks to a group of enthusiastic local craft workers.'

The boundary walls of the estate slide by. The cyclers appear on the towpath up ahead, having travelled upriver to meet me. As I paddle towards Ballingrane lock, a small tin punt shudders against the pier while a man yanks furiously at the outboard's starter cord, his mate hovering on the towpath, sullen and soaking wet. I look up at him questioningly. 'Fell in. Almost got sucked down the sluice trying to fill the lock!' Crikey, I think to myself, there's nothing more unnerving on the water than amateurs messing about in boats. I need to get away from these guys quickly. I slide through the open gate and into the full lock chamber, and hope their engine refuses to start. Too late.

The little outboard wheezes into life and the boat splutters up behind me. The half-drowned man strides down to the far end of the chamber, lock key swinging in his hand. I don't trust this loon anywhere near a sluice gate; he would probably open both sluices fully, which would be disastrous for my canoe. Luckily my father steps in and takes charge, just in the nick of time.

Downstream, the river flows deep and wide through lush countryside, magically devoid of human intervention. This landscape stirs the soul. I only wish Annabel could be here to share the experience. Perhaps we can recreate the adventure next year, or at a time when she feels ready.

The summer heat and clear skies have drawn others to the river – pods of kayakers, dog-walkers, fishermen and swimmers. When I approach the weir at Clashganny, childhood memories rise like milk to the boil. This is where I learned to swim when I was four years old. The broad reach of river bounded on one side by a long cascading weir was our wild infinity pool. Under the umbrella of a giant oak tree, we would change into our swimming togs and slide down the bank into the water. Looking at the faded colour photograph of my four-year-old self, I'm struck by how fearless I appear to be, bathing in waters far beyond my depth. At what point in our lives do anxieties and fears take hold and conspire to hold us back? Back then we always had the place to

'Looking at the faded colour photograph of my four-year-old self, I'm struck by how fearless I appear to be, bathing in waters far beyond my depth.'

ourselves, river swimming being then not as popular as it is today. It's impossible to keep a good thing secret. Soon, more people turned up, wanting in on the beauty spot. In recent times it's become so popular there's even a lifeguard on duty at peak summer times.

I stopped swimming in the Barrow over a decade ago. I was having a dip one midsummer's evening when a human turd floated past. The unpleasant encounter was the result of untreated waste water entering the river upstream. At the time, riverside towns such as Bagenalstown and Carlow were expanding rapidly. The Celtic Tiger was in full swing, and new housing estates popped up seemingly overnight. Archaic urban wastewater treatment plants were unable to cope with the increasing demand, resulting in effluent discharges into the river.

As a natural resource, water has been ripe for exploitation, for extraction, waste disposal and power generation. Since the Industrial Revolution, waterbodies have been placed under serious pressure, and access to the resource has been unregulated. In response to increasing concerns about the decline of Europe's water quality, legislation was introduced in 2000 in the form of the EU Water Framework Directive. The mandate requires the achievement of 'good status' in all water bodies and the prevention of further deterioration. To comply with this directive, the Irish government established a National River Management Plan, setting out the steps required to protect and improve the country's water quality. The Environmental Protection Agency (EPA) is responsible for monitoring and reporting on the quality of Ireland's water, with other public bodies also involved. Water sampling is now carried out on 13,200 kilometres of rivers and streams. Lakes, canals, estuaries, coastal regions and groundwater are also included. All this valuable scientific data establish a picture of the ecological health of Ireland's waterways.

As far as the Barrow is concerned, the increased regulations and monitoring continues to have a positive impact. Serious incidents of pollution rarely occur, most riverside wastewater treatment plants have been upgraded, and the 'slime growths' caused by the Carlow sugar factory are a thing of the past. However, according to the most recent survey of water quality, published by the EPA in 2019, there has been a decline, especially in rivers, with a persistent deterioration of pristine waterways. The principal issue is excessive levels of nitrogen and phosphorous caused largely by agricultural run-off and point-source pollution, with raw sewage at some urban centres. While there is broad acceptance of the causes of pollution and the effect it has on water quality, initiating change is the difficult part, since it inevitably involves conflicting interests and financial sacrifices.

'While there is broad acceptance of the causes of pollution and the effect it has on water quality, initiating change is the difficult part, since it inevitably involves conflicting interests and financial sacrifices.'

Assigning legal status to rivers is a recent phenomenon, reflecting an increasing rights-based approach to environmental protection. In 2017, New Zealand's Whanganui River became the first water body to receive legal recognition as having the same rights, duties and liabilities as a person. The Whanganui Treaty concluded a 140-year campaign by the indigenous Maori Iwi tribe for the return and recognition of tribal lands, of which the river is an integral part. The treaty seeks to preserve the river for future generations of Iwi and all New Zealanders. Since this landmark decision, similar legal status has been accorded to the Rio Atrato in Colombia and the Ganges and Yamuna rivers in India. These rivers now have the right to representation in legal proceedings. Critics of this development argue that it sets a precedent for granting legal rights to a wide range of natural resources, such as forests and mountains, resulting in exposure to lawsuits. Advocates contend that it is an important step in protecting ecosystems on which human life depends. Could this movement herald a new era of veneration for our rivers and waterways? The Celtic druids would no doubt approve.

As I drift past the swimming pier at Clashganny, I am amazed at the activity on the towpath. Families and groups are sprawled alongside, and the narrow path is cluttered with deckchairs and cool-boxes. Gangs of shrieking kids hurl themselves into the water. A few canoes hover around the weir, perhaps considering shooting the falls, so I hove to and watch the entertainment unfold. The first party, an open canoe crewed by three men, approaches the edge of the weir warily. The flow snatches the canoe, hurls it down the face of the weir and capsizes it in the rapids below. Two of the occupants manage to swim ashore, while a third trails the semi-submerged canoe as it disappears downstream. Meanwhile, the two waterproof barrels containing all their camping gear float out of sight. In spite of the chaos, everyone appears to be thoroughly enjoying themselves.

Downriver, away from the crowds, a chain of bubbles breaks the still water. A head surfaces, wet fur, dark-brown, snub-nosed, long whiskers: an otter. I know it's an otter because I've seen one here before. The creature rolls on its back and sinks its teeth into the flesh of the tiny fish clasped in its forepaws. I can't believe my luck, and dare not breathe for fear of scaring it away. Whenever I read about otters, they are described as nocturnal animals, but my otter must be an exception, because I have always encountered it in broad daylight. Otters are also noted for being incredibly shy and furtive, but again this river otter defies the rules, seemingly comfortable with human presence.

For reasons not fully understood, Ireland's otter population is considered to be strong, while in the rest of Europe it's a different story, as otter numbers are in steep decline. In Switzerland and the Netherlands they are already extinct. This Barrow otter is dark and sleek, with a patch of lighter blond fur running from its chin down across its belly. The body is small, about the size of a big domestic cat. It's fascinating to watch this land-based animal move through the water with such effortless ease and agility. So many of the animal's attributes are designed for swimming – big webbed feet, a powerful tail as rudder, and ears and nose that seal shut underwater.

Otters are creatures of mystery and wonder, sliding effortlessly between two worlds, land and water. They feature strongly in ancient Celtic lore, where their name is *madra uisce*, meaning 'water hound'. According to folkloric tales, an otter's skin is believed to have magical properties. Bags were made from the animal's pelt to keep harps dry, and, when used to line the interior of a battle shield, it was believed to afford a warrior extra protection. Otters are known to protect those they favour, and are loyal companions to anchorites. They feature in the *immram* tales of St Brendan and Máel Dúin. When St Brendan encounters Paul the Hermit on a deserted island, he inquires of the man how he manages to survive. The hermit explains that a family of otters takes care of him, delivering fish and bundles of firewood every few days. In the *Voyage of Máel Dúin*, another epic sea-faring tale, the adventurers make landfall on the Island of Otters, where the obliging creatures provide the hungry crew with a bounty of salmon. On the other hand, *The Legend of Dobhar-Chú*, King Otter, is a more sinister tale, describing a larger-than-life beast, half-dog, half-fish, said to have inhabited Glenade Lough in County Leitrim. The story is told of a woman who goes down to the lake edge to wash some clothes. When she fails to return, her husband heads out to look for her and finds her mutilated body by the lakeside with the *dobhar-chú* stretched out asleep beside her. The husband hurries home to fetch a sword and when he returns to the scene, he drives the blade through the animal's chest. The *dobhar-chú* tombstone at Conwall cemetery in Glendale valley is connected to this legendary tale. The flagstone features a carving of an otter-like animal being stabbed with a sword. There have been other sightings of King Otter in that area over the centuries, including one in 1896 that was noted in *The Journal of the Royal Society of Antiquaries of Ireland*, by a Mrs Walkington, who described seeing a creature 'half wolf-dog, half fish'.

Aside from the sheer joy and wonder of watching an otter, that it has taken up residency on this stretch of river reflects positively on the local ecosystem. If the water is good enough for an otter, then maybe it is good enough for me. Injected with hope and joy, I set the canoe down the final flight of locks at Ballykeenan. I paddle on past Graiguenamanagh, where there are plenty of boats, including some hardy live-aboards, none of which look as though they have sailed anywhere in the recent past.

The Barrow is wide, deep and sublime now; its flow is languid and a warm breeze ruffles the surface lightly. A steep wooded valley shrouds the river, screening off and muffling out the world beyond. Mighty oaks and beech, conifers and ash reach up to the ridge, while alder and willow dip down by the water's edge. The towpath is an endless border of wild flowers – purple vetch, flowering water mint, hemp agrimony, valerian, bindweed, mallow, willow herb and balsam. Occasionally the honeyed scent of meadowsweet reaches me midstream. This big, beautiful river is all mine. *Minnow* excels in these waters, streaking along, steady and buoyant. That the voyage is almost over is a prospect I try to suppress.

The last lock is a sea lock; tidal waters lie beyond these gates. Downstream, the Barrow will be joined by two other rivers, the Nore and the Suir, creating a powerful union known as the Three Sisters. I'm apprehensive about what lies beyond the lock gates. Estuaries are new territory for me; tidal waters have a fearsome reputation, with forces that can easily overwhelm a small open canoe.

When the gates creak open, I paddle out into a brave new world. It's a grey and murky world, where the water is clouded and the exposed riverbank is coated in a film of fine mud. The tide is on the ebb and, coupled with the river's natural flow, the canoe accelerates. My instinct is to hug the shore, but the way is littered with boulders and other debris. I'm forced to move out to the middle of the river and hold my own in the powerful ebbing waters.

At a bend in the river a few buildings swim into view – the tall mills and wide quays of St Mullins signify my journey's end. Two silhouetted figures, who may or may not be my parents, are standing at the foot of the slipway. I toss *Minnow*'s bowline ashore, where it is caught by eager hands.

Epilogue

It wasn't, of course, the end. The lure of adventure bore away downstream and I could not resist its pull.

While I drifted down the Barrow, a sketchy plan took shape in the recesses of my mind, a plan that would take me out to sea and far horizons. I had been reading about sea roads, *radhadh na mara*, ancient routes used by saints and early settlers, traders and invaders around Ireland's shoreline. The subject caught and held my interest. Perhaps I could explore these historic ways, island-hop the Atlantic coast, dip in and out of coves and journey up estuaries. I was curious to learn about Maude Delap, who carved out a unique scientific career studying the waters around Valentia Island's shores. The life story of Méiní Dunlevy, Blasket Island nurse and midwife, also intrigued me. Along with other trailblazers, Kate Tyrrell, born in 1863 on Ireland's east coast and the world's first female sea captain, captured my admiration. The wildlife potential would be reason enough to journey. I imagined sighting puffin and porpoise, sun fish and basking shark, leatherback turtle and lion's mane jellyfish – the possibilities made me giddy. For such adventures, though, I would clearly need a much bigger boat.

Minnow had reached the boundaries of her world. My small beloved canoe could take me no further than the tidal waters at St Mullins. Having tended to the accumulation of scrapes and scars below the hull's waterline, I stowed her snugly indoors, at least for the time being. For a while, I toyed with the idea of another building project until I realised my notions were a fraction too ambitious. Inconvenient obstacles quickly raised their ugly heads – time, money, materials, space. But my heart was set on a wooden boat, a little daysailer, something with character that could easily be managed solo.

From the moment I saw her, I knew she would be mine. Once the heavy tarpaulin was peeled away, a beautiful wooden sailboat was revealed: a 'Swallows and Amazons' style, Gunter rigged sloop. The hull, formed of thin overlapping planks fastened together with copper rivets, harked back to the Nordic clinker boat tradition. The pronounced curve of her bow recalled the golden age of the Viking longboats. Sadly, her history had been lost over time as her ownership passed through various hands. It is possible she served time as a passenger ferry; the open interior, taken up with four wide benches, has ample room for at least eight people, but I can only guess her story.

Her looks and timeless style appealed to me greatly. The lapped boards, enhanced by layers of varnish, gave off a richly honeyed glow. Her stem, from bow to stern, was painted a bright lapis blue. At some stage a bowsprit had been added, though it appears to be an unfinished afterthought because there is no means of attaching a sail. Set in place, it looked like a battering ram and increased the boats warrior-like air. That she was being offered for sale, fully equipped – mast, sails, rigging, a pair of oars and a robust trailer – clinched the deal.

I have called her *The Pearl* in honour of Jane W. Shackleton, the nineteenth-century photographer, whose custom-built vessel was likewise named.

A long list of chores needed to be tackled before sailing trials. Broken fittings were replaced, new sheets and halyards added, canvas sails restitched and some copper rivets renewed. My vocabulary of sailboat parts was slow to recall – topping lift, vang, snap shackles and cam cleats – words that tripped off the tongue in my earlier sailing days, but had lapsed from memory in the intervening years. The final and strangest of tasks involved flooding the interior with water to encourage the planks to swell. Time spent dry docked had caused the wood to shrink and gaps had appeared along the hull's lapped joints. Failure to soak her thoroughly would result in a nasty surprise and furious bailing on the vessel's maiden sail, I had been warned.

I chose the flattest, calmest day to launch, so calm that I had to row out well beyond the harbour walls in search of the faintest breeze. Under listless sails I watched and waited until silver-backed ripples danced my way. A whisper of wind approached. Rigid with tension, I had forgotten how to breathe. With left hand gripping the gunnel and right hand clasped around the tiller, the sails filled, the hull heeled and *The Pearl* came alive.

'We're sailing! We're sailing!' I shrieked aloud, though there was no one around to hear.

I remained not far from shore on our first sail, short tacks back and forth across the narrow bay and some gentle downwind glides. Enough time, enough wind, for *The Pearl* to reveal some encouraging traits – she was light, strong and swift, capable, I think – I hope – of traversing lakes and estuaries, and of short coastal hops.

The promise of adventure grows ever more real. I can't wait to see where the wild waters take me next.

SELECTED READINGS

Boase, Tessa, *Mrs Pankhurst's Purple Feather: Fashion, Fury and Feminism – Women's Fight for Change* (Aurum Press, 2018)

Colwell, Mary, *Curlew Moon* (William Collins, 2018)

Corlett, Christiaan, *Jane W. Shackleton's Ireland* (The Collins Press, 2012)

Delaney, Ruth, *Inland Waterways* (The Appletree Press, 1986)

Delaney, Ruth, *The Grand Canal of Ireland* (David and Charles Holdings Ltd, 1973)

Devery, Caitriona, *The Story of Brickmaking in Pollagh, County Offaly* (Pollagh Heritage Group, 2019)

Heery, Stephen, *The Shannon Floodlands: A Natural History* (Tir Eolas, 1993)

Irvine, Lucy, *Castaway* (Victor Gollancz, 1983)

Kulczycki, Chris, *The Canoe Shop* (Ragged Mountain Press, 2001)

Landreth, Jenny, *Swell: A Waterbiography* (Bloomsbury, 2018)

Laurie, Marie and Annette Meldrum, *The Borris Lace Collection: A Unique Irish Needlelace* (Sally Milner Publishing Pty Ltd, 2010)

Laverty, Maura, *Never No More* (First published by Longmans, 1942, reprinted Virago Press, 1985)

Lawrence, Tom, *Water Beetles of Pollardstown Fen* (Field Recording, CD, Gruenrekorder, 2011)

Mac Coitir, Niall, *Ireland's Animals: Myths, Legends and Folklore* (The Collins Press, 2010)

Mac Coitir, Niall, *Ireland's Birds: Myths, Legends and Folklore* (The Collins Press, 2015)

Malet, Hugh, *Voyage in a Bowler Hat* (Hutchinson and Co., 1960)

O'Regan, Edward, *In Irish Waterways* (Currach Press, 2005)

Palmer, Eddie and Tony Monaghan, *Irish Canoe Classics: Thirty-Four Great Canoe & Kayak Trips* (Pesda Press, 2011)

Pyle, Hilary, *Red-Headed Rebel, Susan L. Mitchell Poet and Mystic of the Irish Cultural Renaissance* (The Woodfield Press, 1998)

Severin, Tim, *The Brendan Voyage* (Hutchinson & Co. Ltd, 1978)

Sutherland, Audrey, *Paddling North* (Patagonia Books, 2012)

Ward, Mary, *Sketches with the Microscope in a Letter to a Friend* (Brosna Press, 2019, reproduced from the original edition of 1857)

Waterways Guides

Lough Erne Activity Map and Navigation Guide (Ordnance Survey of Northern Ireland with the assistance of Waterways Ireland)

Shannon–Erne Blueway Guide, *Leitrim Village to Belturbet and Crom* (Waterways Ireland)

Shannon Blueway Guides, *Drumshanbo to Carrick-on-Shannon, Carrick-on-Shannon to Lanesborough, Camlin River Loop* (Waterways Ireland)

Guide to the Grand Canal (Waterways Ireland in Association with the Inland Waterways Association of Ireland)

Guide to the River Barrow (Waterways Ireland in Association with the Inland Waterways Association of Ireland)

www.bluewaysireland.org

www.waterwaysireland.org

Acknowledgements

Grateful thanks to: Neil Burkey, Maeve Convery, Conor Graham, Conor Holbrook, Annabel Konig, Wendy Logue, Manchán Magan, Ray Murray, Patrick O'Donoghue, Mandy Parslow, Paddy and Anne Wilkinson, and Jonathan Williams.